I0118085

# Ponder My Thoughts

*(ON THE SOCIAL, ECONOMIC AND THE POLITICAL SCENE IN SIERRA LEONE)*

AN ANTHOLOGY OF WEEKLY THOUGHTS

## Vol. 1

## Andrew Keili

**Sierra Leonean Writers Series**

# Ponder My Thoughts – Vol. 1

ISBN: 978-99910-921-3-3

**Sierra Leonean Writers Series**
Mallam O. & J. Enterprises
120 Kissy Road, Freetown; Warima, Sierra Leone
Publisher: Prof. Osman Sankoh (Mallam O.)
www.sl-writers-series.org
publisher@sl-writers-series.org

# FOREWORD

# BY HON. MR. JUSTICE EDMOND COWAN

"To consolidate Peace after war is a long-term process; to consolidate democracy is an even longer one. There are no quick fixes. Ultimately, consolidating P e a c e in any country depends on the people of that country. They alone must determine the path to peace – the international community can only assist" - (Lakhdar Brahimi, former Foreign Minister of Algeria).

"Ponder my Thoughts" is described by the Author as "An anthology of weekly Newspaper articles written o n various facets of the political, social and economic scene in Sierra Leone. It captures many of the issues affecting t h e daily lives of people in Sierra Leone. It provides a critique of political and governance issues, sometimes providing a detailed analysis of problems encountered that will provide guidance to the reader on the problems confronting a developing country like Sierra Leone. This also extends to issues of the economy. Sierra Leone is a country w i t h m a ny ethnic groupings and people in various works of life and religious settings, sometimes with startling and humorous results. These upheavals are also captured in the Book."

"Ponder my Thoughts" is a must read, as it provides both international and national actors with comprehensive, practical guidance, on designing, implementing, supporting, and attempting to address the factors that have fed conflict in the past.

These collection of newspaper articles would be useful to various categories of people and international organizations who may want to develop and improve on the assistance that can be made available to communities emerging from conflict like Sierra Leone, in the areas of security and stabilization, elections and political reconciliation, Human rights and Judicial reform, institution-building, Governance and the re-energising of social and economic development.

This book "Ponder my Thoughts" is a welcome toolbox at the disposal of National and International Organisations as well as Governments involved in post conflict nation building. It is especially commendable because it does not provide one-size-fits-all solutions to what are highly political and sensitive processes each with their own unique challenges and opportunities.

The Author's effort is laudable because he has drawn not only upon his own extensive experience, but also upon that of many others from across the country and beyond. These collections of newspaper articles reminds the reader that historic, cultural, institutional, ethnic and linguistic differences among citizens will lead to different outcomes; no two processes are alike and no single model will necessarily lead to the hoped-for result-the variables are too great. The stakes may be highest here because the outcome will determine how power and resources are shared. Despite the complexity of the subject matter the author briefly raises the practical issues and concerns that people in Governance should consider at each stage, and identifies the core Institutions and tasks of policy making and the risks and opportunities associated with each. Ending a conflict and rebuilding state institutions and a society torn apart by civil war are highly delicate tasks. This is more evident in the

Governance process, where the past must be examined and agreements reached between other mistrustful citizens and communities.

"Ponder my Thoughts", a collection of weekly thoughts is an important and welcome tool for International actors and National actors alike: it will enrich a learning process as we seek to improve our efforts to secure peace and transform communities.

**E.K. Cowan**

**Ombudsman of Sierra Leone**

# January 3, 2013

## MISUSE OF DONOR FUNDS

Misuse of donor funds is nothing new but the recent case of the GAVI funds, prudent use of which could have done so much to address childhood health problems, should gall anyone who cares about this in Sierra Leone. The real truth is yet to be unearthed but the misuse of donor funds has been going on unchecked in many sectors. Usually a structure should be set up for managing programmes but it seems like it is these very structures that are undermined. The relationship of these programmes with line ministries seems to vary from programme to programme. Most of these programmes are also monitored by donors and reported upon in the reports of their supervision missions. It is surprising how many startling revelations are made in these reports for which there is no follow-up. It seems the follow up only becomes important when donors threaten to withdraw funds. It also surprises me that ministers would seem to distance themselves from such when problems arise. When the problem occurs over a sustained period, the management skills of the minister have got to be questioned. The Gavi fund debacle is being investigated. One very much hopes the investigations will be dispassionate and remedial measures will be taken and that we can learn not to repeat the mistakes with other programmes.

## REGULATING THE ELECTRICITY SECTOR

One might be excused for sympathising with any Minister of Energy. Getting the electricity sector from its less than 10% access rate nationally to any meaningful figure is indeed a yeoman's task. While the long-term plans for future power provision are being put in place, and whilst experiencing problems with the power output from the current Bumbuna

Phase 1, an Independent Power provider (IPP) project could indeed be welcome. As long as this is done in a transparent way and specified properly with recourse to reducing the cost of production, it will be welcome news. It is however surprising that even though an Act has been passed to set up a regulatory agency for the electricity and water sectors, this has not been effected. The advantages of having a regulator are many. It will help both the power provider and the consumer, resulting in better power provision. The regulatory agency will ensure that tariffs charged are fair and that there is healthy competition between the providers. It will also ensure that the inefficiencies of the provider and/or the National Power Authority (NPA) are not passed on to the consumer. Time for the government to act fast on the regulatory agency!

## MINIMISING ROAD CONSTRUCTION INCONVE-NIENCE

The advantages of new roads projects cannot be disputed and any well-meaning citizen would welcome a well-conceived and executed road project. Roads open up new areas for development, facilitate our movement and result overall in economic development. It should be unreasonable to expect that these projects cannot proceed without some inconvenience to users. What is however surprising is the almost cocky attitude of construction companies who could care less about inconveniencing people for prolonged periods. Countless people have gone without electricity and water because of the roads projects, as cables and pipes are moved for unduly long periods. This needs better liaison between the road construction companies and the utility companies. It is irritating that road companies do not even bother to put up signs for road diversions. Drivers have been forced to get themselves into corners sometimes with unwelcome results. Hazardous areas like gaping holes are not even marked and one could keep going round in circles if you cannot discern the correct detour. Surely with a little bit of thought these problems can be sorted out. It is no excuse to say they are so busy with the construction that they cannot be bothered with "small matters". In any case all road companies are required by law to prepare an Environmental Management Plan which addresses such issues. These are not mundane — they can save lives and obviate unnecessary inconvenience. Time for the Sierra Leone Roads Authority (SLRA) to get tough!

## WELCOMING PARLIAMENTARY OVERSIGHT CO-MMITTEES

Parliament has been busy setting up committees to provide oversight of the functioning of various ministries. This is good as it provides an alternative oversight of these ministries from our lawmakers. After all they make the laws by which these ministries function. One however wonders about the effectiveness of some of these committees which seem to acquiesce to the whims of the institutions under these ministries. One wonders whether with an effective oversight Committee for the Health Sector, a problem like the Gavi fund issue could not have been averted. Oversight committees should not be used as intimidating tools for the purpose of getting favours for the members. Oversight committees must probe but not be so interventionist as if they run these institutions. This is a new Parliament with ostensibly a lot of bright new people, many of them professionals, who have made their mark in various spheres of work before becoming lawmakers. Here's hoping that we will have more effective oversight committees.

Ponder my thoughts.

# February 10, 2013

## THE NEW CABINET - PW IS KEY

One thing is clear about the new Cabinet appointments — President Koroma can make or break. It really does not matter whether the "making and breaking" is considered illogical, he has used his absolute powers to appoint people he considers appropriate for the various positions. There were obviously some surprises and one can be excused for not being quite certain what his overriding considerations might have been. The exclusion of some of those considered good performers like I.B. Kargbo, Soccoh Kabia and Steven Gaojia would give the impression that past performance was not necessarily key to getting reappointed. If I should hazard a guess, I would say that his appointments so far have been based on political payback, loyalty, regional considerations and the need to satisfy various interest groups, probably with an eye on anchoring his party firmly for 2017.

To many people for whom competence and performance are key, the appointments were disappointing as many of the poor performers, even by the government's own yardstick — the evaluation of the performance contract of ministers, and Open Government Initiative (OGI) assessments etc. — were retained. The appointments of Kaifala Marah and Samura Kamara have been generally well received as seasoned hands who would man their ministries well. By appointing 'young Turks' such as Miatta Kargbo at Health and Momodu Maligi at Water Resources, he has not only sought to placate the youth constituency but managed to satisfy other considerations. Moijueh Kaikai, Musa Tarawalli, J.B. Dauda and Diana Konomanyi help make for a fairly palatable regional spread to cover the non-traditional strongholds of the South and the East. Only Kailahun and Bo have thus far not had a representation at the cabinet level. He has also retained a host of allies many of whom were very instrumental in the party's retention of power and has chosen ministers from every one of the Northern districts and the Western Area. He has also in one stroke cut the legs off the People's Movement for Democratic Change (PMDC) and attempted to make forays into Sierra Leone People's Party (SLPP) territory. Time will tell whether he is the Grand master at this game of chess.

The appointments have not been as earth shattering as people initially thought. The fact that three months after the elections, the president has not completed his appointments is also disappointing to many who consider his seeming indecision as a sign of not being convinced and resolute enough about what he is doing. The silence on the filling of the remaining ministerial vacancies is baffling. Whatever one's views are on the cabinet, one thing is clear in a country like this-the performance of the Cabinet ministers will also to a large extent depend on the Political Will of the president. That big PW!

Ministers serve at his pleasure and he can remove them at any time, based on performance assessments or some other criteria which need not be explicit. He has already —from veiled threats to remove "non-performers" — hung the sword of Damocles over their heads. They will, no doubt, after the delays in their appointments, and threats, thank God for small mercies. Also government policy in many areas has been laid down and is quite unequivocal, with a considerable number of technocrats and administrators in the ministries to assist with the work of the ministers and with deputy ministers sometimes thrown in for good measure. Donors who deal with these ministries are also often quite clear about the direction of whatever assistance they may give.

Whatever the competence of the minister, or his proclivity to veer in certain directions, the political will of both the minister and the president in my view overrides everything else. If the inclination is to serve the country well and put her above self, things will work out. If President Koroma intends to leave a commendable legacy for his stewardship of the country, especially during a second term without encumbrances, he will be able to do so. Whatever our political differences, we will also be looking forward to such a stewardship. Will the new ministers lay good eggs? The jury is out.

## NEW ANGLICAN BISHOP

Not many people know that the Anglican Church will be electing a new bishop on February 22nd. Traditional churches have undergone a sustained period of atrophy with members taking off in droves for Pentecostal churches. A considerable number of initiatives have been undertaken during Bishop Julius Lynch's tenure but the time has now come to pass on the baton as he retires later this year. The Anglican Church is very wide in latitude from "High Church Anglo Catholic" to "Evangelical" to "Charismatic" leanings. It also has considerable latitude in interpreting its doctrines. The new bishop will be faced with a considerable number of challenges and some would say the church has to "reform or die".

The church that founded the Church Mission Society (CMS) Grammar School and Annie Walsh Memorial School, played a yeoman's role in the early formative years of Fourah Bay College, and was once the "Official State Church" is faced with a serious decision. Apart from his spiritual duties, the new bishop will also be very instrumental in shaping many aspects of national life from proffering views on governance to making decisions on church-owned land etc. Considering that a bishop retires at 70, it is not inconceivable that a young bishop might be in office for some 20 to 30 years, if one is chosen. This is indeed a weighty decision.

Whatever the choice, character will also be important. The Apostle Paul in 1 Timothy 3:2-7 states the qualification for being a bishop thus:

Bishop must be above reproach, the husband but one wife, temperate, self controlled, respectable, hospitable, able to teach, not given to drunkenness, not violent but gentle, not quarrelsome, not a lover of money…He must also have a good reputation with outsiders, so that he will not fall into disgrace and into the devil's trap."

This is true now as it was true in the first century. As I join the other delegates at a special Synod meeting to vote for our new bishop, I pray that God will appoint a suitable leader amongst the three candidates, Canons Emerson Thomas, Thomas Wilson, and Kweku Hagan, to lead the Church through these troubled times. Please pray for us and wish us well.

Ponder my thoughts.

# February 18, 2013

## THE ANNIE WALSH "MARKET"

The furore surrounding the Annie Walsh relocation has shed light on a considerable number of issues. All groups concerned have had their own share of criticism. I was taken aback by scathing criticism from an avid Anglican of the senior Anglican priest, who was "outed" in the letter of clarification from the secretary to the president, Osho Coker:

"I will not allow the names of our President, Government, and APC Party to be muddied because of one greedy individual. Government must identify and name that Senior Anglican Priest who in fact is a Judas, a betrayer, a traitor and an enemy of Anglicanism and Jesus Christ, so we can quickly crucify him during this Lenten season."

Strong unforgiving words indeed! For me there are a few lessons I have learnt from the behaviour of the various parties.

The Anglican Church: The Church probably now realises the advantage of singing from the same hymn sheet — being careful with unauthorised statements made on its behalf and consulting well with the Annie Walsh Old Girls Association (AWOGA) and other associated groups. As much as the church is custodian of the property, decisions of this magnitude involve a multiplicity of stakeholders, not least AWOGA members who hold the school so dear to their hearts.

The Annie Walsh Old Girls Association (AWOGA): It is obvious that the school relocation issue may not have been well thought through or even if it was, such information was not well disseminated to the rank and file of the old girls. Do they plan to move to Regent? When? What happens at the existing premises considering the need to preserve the school's monumental value and rich heritage? How will the project be funded? Do they need government's help?

Government: The government appears to have shrewdly deflected the situation and the "Senior Anglican clergyman" has been hung out to dry. A closer examination would however indicate that the government was less concerned with preserving the school's monumental value and heritage.

In the Secretary to the President's letter, he states: "…the land vacated at Kissy Road will then be utilized for the construction of a modern market to be occupied by traders that are being removed from the streets of Freetown".

It is only in his second letter that he alludes to the preservation of the school's heritage when he states: "...such reaction could include concerns about the preservation of the monumental value of some of the buildings housing the school..."
Very clever indeed! Who wants to be chased by those AWOGA women?

For now it would seem like the "Annie Walsh market" issue is behind us. It has however left in its wake an "outed" senior Anglican clergyman, a discordant old girls association, a confused church and a clever government that does not want to incur the wrath of the Old Girls. Everyone has now gone home with tails between their legs. At least for now!

## ELECTRICTY WITHOUT "INSOLENCE"

I was bemused to read statements made by the Honourable Alpha Kanu, minister of information, and some journalists sympathetic to the government, on the matter of Lawyer Jenkins Johnston's Open letter to the President on the "appalling" electricity situation.

One publication claims that Minister Kanu referred to Jenkins Johnston's outburst as "very insolent" and claimed that he had in fact insulted the president. He went on to say "Where was Jenkins-Johnston when the Sierra Leone People's Party was generating 3 Mega-watts of electricity and the entire country was in total darkness? He seems to be suffering from selective amnesia."

Someone in an article gave his opinion on this the issue better than I could.

"Surrogates are trying to mute genuine observations and well-substantiated criticisms... I would rather see a public expression of frustration and anger in a letter rather than, God forbid, frustration and anger leading to conflagration and widespread destruction."

The government needs to realize that sometimes bringing things in the open may even assist in assuaging the fears of the public. What is wrong if the government goes beyond its prepared script of merely stating there is a breakdown at Bumbuna and explains to the public about the problems with Bumbuna, plans afoot to bring on more electricity through Independent Power Providers (IPPs), plans to address the transmission and distribution problems etc? This can only be good for the public which, after all has its own share of the blame as many people who complain refuse to pay their bills. Government should be about openness. The right of all persons to ask public officials for information should not be stifled. If the questions are not being answered perhaps it is not such a bad idea if it is publicised as Jenkins Johnston has done. One may argue that when professional and civil society organizations either stay mute, or are accused of being politically motivated when they do, a prominent citizen speaking out is not a bad thing.

As for Hon. Alpha Kanu's disparaging reference to past performance by the previous government, it is really high time we moved forward. Incessantly referencing yesteryears for point scoring does not help the situation and does not bring any gain.

If we are to progress as a nation we have to constantly strive to improve upon the present. Let's face it, as much as we may appreciate strides made by government we have to admit that we should try to markedly improve upon our low infrastructure provision indices. Pointing these out does not mean the government's efforts are not appreciated. Who knows? Even President Koroma may want to get more clarity on the issues.

Regarding Hon. Kanu's reference to Jenkins Johnston's "Sunday school manners" I can only remind him that Christ himself was very scathing when speaking the truth. In Matthew 23:25 he says: "Woe to you, scribes and Phasisees, you hypocrites! For you cleanse the outside of the cup and of the plate, but inside they are full of extortion and rapacity." Tak about strong medicine. Talk about strong language. Talk about laying down the gauntlet. Talk about call a spade a spade. Jenkins Johnston's statement was kid's stuff in comparison.

Ponder my thoughts.

# February 25, 2013

## PITY OUR UNEMPLOYED GRADUATES

An oft ignored problem is that of graduate unemployment. If you are an employer like me you will have stacks of CVs of recently qualified graduates in disciplines ranging from engineering and accounting to peace and conflict studies. All the job hopefuls have one forlorn hope — that they will land a job, any job. The graduate unemployment problem is so enormous that whatever help one could offer directly through actually looking for job openings or merely offering advice on possibilities would be a drop in the ocean.

One does not know about any government or private-sector programmer that attempts to address this problem in a concerted way. The youth ministry and Youth Commission acknowledge this problem but beyond mere rhetoric the actuality of addressing the problem seems remote.

The education and labor ministries can't keep relevant statistics let alone attempt to address the problem. The private sector does its own share of absorption but this merely scratches the surface. How many financial and business services graduates can the banks or other financial services organisations absorb? How many engineers can the mining companies or infrastructure projects employ? What happens to the graduates in the Arts, social sciences and peace and conflict studies? The reality is that the civil service is bloated and the capacity of ministries, departments and agencies (MDAs) to absorb graduates is severely limited. The problem is serious but then our universities and colleges continue to churn out these bright hopeful young people in their numbers every year.

The Local Content Policy if well implemented will help. The private sector will take in some people but this is woefully inadequate in addressing the problem. What we need is a concerted government programme that encompasses the participation and collaboration between various ministries — education, labor and employment, and youth ministries in particular. Tackling the problem obviously requires them to build a nexus with other ministries like trade and industry (spearheading the local content initiative), employers and universities and colleges. They may want to answer the following questions: Are courses offered relevant for the job market? Do they keep relevant statistics on recent graduate students? Do they have job placement programmes? Do they seek the views of various employers on the relevance of courses and performance of graduates? Do graduates need some sort of postgraduate crash training to prepare them for the job market?

To my mind the expansion of the private sector will go a long way towards addressing the problem. With 70 percent of the economy in the informal sector there is considerable scope for expanding the formal private sector with the right policies. A major new initiative could be in the area of internships. Encouraging companies to have one-year internship programmes for graduates and training them for the job market whilst paying them a stipend could be a good way to go. Companies will however be loathe to implement such a scheme unless they are given some sort of incentive; granting them tax incentives may not be such a bad idea.

The logical question is what happens after such a programme. First, they will be better prepared for the job market. Second if they are trained in entrepreneurship skills they may be able to fan out on their own. Also if the employer wishes to expand his operations he has a ready pool of workers to choose from.

The government should put on its thinking cap, think out of the box and get someone to spearhead this endeavour.

# THE PRESIDENT ON NATIONAL COHESION

I was not surprised at the inordinate amount of time devoted to political tolerance and national cohesion in the president's speech during his swearing-in ceremony in November immediately after the election results were announced. President Koroma seems to have continued his rhetoric in last week's inauguration speech. I reproduce below relevant excerpts from this speech.

"This is the time for all of us to embrace each other. In the name of Mama Sierra Leone, let all APC supporters embrace every SLPP supporter and supporters of other political parties."
"...I will make sure that the fruits of the Agenda for Prosperity are equally distributed in every district and region of the country."
"...every Sierra Leonean, from all political parties, regions, ethnic group, age, and religion is central to our Agenda for Prosperity. We must therefore embrace each other........"
"....prosperous Sierra Leone, whose sons and daughters will live together in peace and harmony, and enjoy the abundant fruits of our labour."
The one I like best for its prose is "Fellow Sierra Leoneans, democracy respects divisions; good governance transcends divisions"

Impressive rhetoric, indeed!

Three months after the elections government is slowly putting together the team to manage the affairs of state. Some might say that, whatever one's views may be about the competence or suitability of the appointees, in terms of nationwide representation, ministerial appointments were not skewed in regional or tribal terms. A lot more appointments would need to be made — ambassadors, board chairmen and other board members, appointments to government agencies etc. One only hopes that in such appointments, apart from overriding criteria based on merit, consideration be given to not making such appointments so overtly skewed as to give the impression that we have a divided country. As the president himself has said "Democracy respects divisions, good governance transcends divisions."

I was somehow heartened to learn that two of the recent appointments to important specialised positions in agencies/programmes seem to have been based on merit even though the holders do not come from traditional ruling party strongholds. One to head the National Minerals Agency and the other is spearheading the Millennium Challenge Corporation (MCC) initiative. These are two of the country's finest brains with whom I have worked and who will undoubtedly contribute positively to the Agenda for Prosperity.

Other government appointments will be made soon and one hopes that this practice of meritocracy will continue, irrespective of people's origins. On the negative side, I find it difficult to believe rumours that the reason Sierra Leone Roads Authority (SLRA) is cash starved, unable to meet their operational commitments and staff have not been paid for over two months may be based on the fact that far too many of the senior people are from the "wrong part of the country". Surely this cannot happen under the Agenda for Prosperity!

We will undoubtedly also wait and see if the culture of meritocracy will be imbibed into the functioning of ministries, departments and agencies (MDAs) and parastatals, which have been accused in the past of unfair employment practices and political witch hunts. As the president himself has said "the time for politics is over". Surrogates beware! As for sharing the national cake, it is reassuring to note from the budget speech that projects seem to be distributed fairly evenly round the country. Let us hope that the associated contracts will also be distributed based on performance and merit. The allocations to local councils also seem to have followed the same fate. Let us hope the government practises meaningful decentralisation and devolution of functions, holding the hands of the local councils to the fire for non performance irrespective of location. There may be initial promising signs but the jury is still out.

Ponder my thoughts.

# March 2, 2013

## "SOLO B"- BEST PRESIDENT THAT NEVER WAS?

One does not have to be close to former vice president and presidential aspirant of the SLPP Honourable Solomon Berewa "Solo B" to know that he is still reeling from the outcome of the 2007 presidential elections. Those who he purports to have been complicit in his defeat like Dr. Christiana Thorpe and President Kabbah would obviously be expected to feature prominently in his long awaited book "A New Perspective on Governance, Leadership, Conflict and Nation building in Sierra Leone" which was launched at the British Council on Wednesday, February 28th, 2013. He has not disappointed.

Solo B espouses his views on these significant issues whilst citing Sierra Leone's leaders from independence to now to make his case. As would be expected he does not mince his words when assessing our various leaders, liberally putting his share of blame for our predicament on these leaders.

Those who know Solo B know he takes no prisoners. His detractors accuse him of vindictiveness, being ungrateful to President Kabbah and wallowing too much on the vote cancellation issue by Christiana Thorpe. His role in many other issues like the Hinga Norman incarceration, the treason trials, Charles Margai's defection, as well as his choice of running mate, who many say was "foisted" on him are deftly handled in the book. I will leave readers to be the judge of whether he addresses supposedly negative perceptions well.

I will however dwell on what I know about Solo B and how this seems to be borne out in this book. I have known him in his capacity as the president of the CKC Old Boys Association (COBA) and as vice president. I know him as an urbane, deeply religious man, thorough in what he does, and one who eschews bigotry. He was known for his attention to detail and quick grasp of issues during his tenure as vice president. The hard work he put into resolving the Bubuakei Jabbi court case before the last SLPP flagbearer election illustrates both his attention to detail and evenhandedness in dealing with issues. I do know from his handling of appointments during his tenure as vice president that he favoured competent people and from his involvement in SLPP peace talks that he is very measured and fair in his approach.

I would like to highlight a few excerpts from the book to illustrate these virtues.

**A patriot with a penchant for religious fervour:** Solo B could have marshalled supporters to protest the results of the elections and whip up a frenzy that could have resulted in violence and division of the country but he chose not to.

*first line of the prayer of St Francis, "Oh Lord make me an instrument of your peace"…. Strengthened to pursue the course of peace…It helped me make up my mind that the best course of action was to demonstrate good leadership…and to advise my numerous supporters who were then teeming around me to have faith and to realise that right is might… and that with faith they should all at that moment, dare to do their best and their duty for their country and their people as they understood it"*

**A man of conviction:** He has always stood up against what he thought was not legally right, especially the nullification of results from some polling stations against constitutional and legal provisions.

*Electoral Commissioner would of course say that at the time she declared the results of the run-off election her conscience was clear about her invalidating 169,054 votes cast on my behalf at the 477 polling stations which she invalidated as containing excess votes. Of course every person's conscience can be clear if that person sets a low standard for his or her conscience to follow. This was exactly what the Chief Electoral Commissioner of Sierra Leone did in the election of 2007."*

**Loyal. Swift to chide and swift to bless**: He has made several scathing remarks about President Kabbah which make interesting reading, detailing how an initial friendship and mutual respect changed to distrust. Through all of this he was loyal.

Despite this he seems to take a more realistic stand on the issue in his postscript.

*remember him as a good friend because he seemed to treat me so. This was of course when he needed my services. At that time he would lead me through the garden path showering much praises on me. When he no longer needed my services he would abandon me in the lurch. This might not be typical of the man."*

**A nationalist who is not bigoted**. He evenly apportions the blame for the country's ills and identifies Sir Albert Margai as the one who stated bringing tribal considerations into politics.

*"Albert Margai became the first person who constituted a turning point in the democratic process Sierra Leone had embarked upon under Sir Milton Margai. He was not particularly keen to promote national cohesion, but only to enhance his grip on power. Thus he started to rekindle the now forgotten north and south and Mende-Temne political divide and rivalry. That rivalry has unfortunately persisted ever since and it has been manifested itself in different forms especially in times of political contests."*

**Respect for Authority:** It is his relationship with President Koroma that appears strange to many partisans.

*always been and I am still on good terms with the incumbent President--as President he has always treated me with respect and decorum whenever we meet. He demonstrates this by occasional telephone calls he makes to me asking after my well being. I appreciate those calls... I hope that this will be an enduring mark of his presidency".*

The question one would like to ask is how would a President Berewa have steered the ship of state? He has espoused good ideas on governance, leadership, conflict and nation building which future leaders can learn from; lessons from history are particularly pertinent. Is Berewa the best President we never had? Ponder his writings and his character and be the judge.

## NP "PASS ALL"

There is often scepticism in Sierra Leone about privatisation of local companies. It is often the case that many a privatisation has gone awry because of a mixture of reasons including problems with entrenched interests, poor restructuring of the company, continued government interference and poor corporate governance and management.

It is therefore heartening to note that the recipient of the award for Outstanding Performance in the Industry category given by the Serra Leone Chamber of Commerce Industry and Agriculture was National Petroleum Sierra Leone Limited (NP-SL Ltd). The award was presented by President Koroma at this year's Chamber dinner held in the House of Parliament. NP has been an industry leader in the downstream petroleum sector since its early days with its antecedent companies British Petroleum and AGIP Oil Company. It has recently undergone a rebranding, revitalization and expansion programme of its operation in Sierra Leone and the sub region. It has remodeled its existing stations, established operations in Liberia and contemplates establishing operations in Senegal and Guinea. Not bad for a Sierra Leonean company! NP (SL) Ltd. still maintains its position as the leading supplier of petroleum products in Sierra Leone.

For a company in which government divested its 60 percent shares predominantly to Leoneoil, and with a local management and a corporate structure, to successfully follow through on an unmatched vision of competing in the West African sub region is indeed commendable. Well done, NP. Indeed, NP "Pass all"!

Ponder my thoughts.

# March 11, 2013

## SALUTING THE NATIONAL MINERALS AGENCY

I lost a bet recently and I am glad I did. The bet was that the government would not establish the National Minerals Agency (NMA) for the simple reason that the agency would take an inordinate amount of authority from the Ministry of Mines and Minerals Resources (MMR). After all turkeys don't vote for Christmas! The NMA was finally launched last week by the president. Congratulations to the government.

Lest the government revels in this, I would like to register my disappointment at the Extractive Industries Transparency Initiative (EITI) setback. After so much hoopla, Sierra Leone has been suspended from the EITI for non-compliance in its requirements. Simply put, the EITI has found that there is a lot left to be desired in the area of transparency in the extractives sector. I listened to the new minister of finance's statement at the NMA launching. He seemed visibly irked by the inimical role played by various players in this saga. According to him, the recipients of payments at the local level, ministries, departments and agencies (MDAs) dealing with the sector, and mining companies, all had a share of the blame. His anger is understandable as he was the EITI champion when he was chief of staff at State House. He says steps have been put in place to prevent a recurrence, including the setting up of a desk at the National Revenue Authority (NRA) dedicated to receiving and reconciling payments for the extractives sector. Whatever the case, the government needs to take the blame for the EITI debacle especially after so much publicity about setting up systems that would make access to mineral industry payments public.

Now back to the National Minerals Agency. The NMA will be a highly professional unit ensuring effective, consistent management of mineral rights, geological information and regulated precious minerals trading. A reformed Ministry of Mines and Mineral Resources (MMR) will only have responsibility for legislation, policy formulation, and oversight. The NMA has been well set up and the initial recruitments sound promising. Also on the positive side, the president, finance minister, and the mines and mineral resources minister all reiterated their support for this venture at the launching. However, cautionary notes sounded by representatives of the various donors — the World Bank, the European Union (EU), the Deutsche Gesellschaft für Internationale Zusammenarbeit GmbH or GIZ, and U.K.'s Department for International Development (Dfid) — about the need for government to restructure the MMR to meet its changed mandate, the need for government to ensure that assistance to the NMA was sustainable, and for cooperation and respect between the NMA and MMR seemed to raise a red flag. Political will is obviously key to the NMA's success.

On another note there seem to be some positive developments in the mining sector. In his recent budget speech the minister of finance stated that a comprehensive Extractive Industries Revenue Bill has been drafted to manage the country's mining and petroleum fiscal regimes. This spells out all the taxes, levies and charges that are applicable to mining and petroleum activities. A Mining Resource Rent Tax and a Petroleum Resource Rent Tax are proposed in the bill, the objective of which is to enable government derive additional tax revenues from these activities, in the event profits are above projections — a sort of windfall tax. It is also proposed to establish a Transformation Fund, where a portion of all mineral and petroleum tax and non-tax revenues will be deposited. This fund will be a part of the Consolidated Revenue Fund so that all revenues flow through the government budget. This will ensure that revenues from our natural resources are used prudently and in a transparent manner. Government is also working on a fiscal rule to define the proportion of revenues that will be used in any given year in such a way that government expenditures remain stable, sustainable and predictable over time.

On paper these are good steps that address many of the criticisms more recently levied at the government for the mining sector, which would lead to better management of our mineral resources. Let us hope that this time government will muster the political will to seriously address the problems of the sector. We will however wait to see how well these are implemented. As has been seen from the EITI, government needs to both talk the talk and walk the walk.

## OBITUARY FOR TENNIS IN SIERRA LEONE

I wasn't exactly a tennis prodigy during my younger days but I did hold my own against tough opposition and played at national level. Unfortunately my cupboard, which was full of tennis trophies for various local and national tournaments, was emptied by rebels during the attack on Sierra Rutile. Alright, so the old bones do creak now and I occasionally (actually frequently) discover muscles I didn't know existed when I attempt to play as I have been doing recently at the Hill Station club after a protracted absence. I hope this will bring down the bulge and the beer belly.

Seriously though, every time I visit the club and play with the young and not-so-young players, I lament the decline of tennis in this country. I have a soft spot for my tennis mates - a potpourri of people ranging from fairly affluent businessmen and professionals to young, mostly ill-educated boys who started off as ball boys. Many of these have become lifelong friends. I still recall with fondness the champions of old like Rudi Dworzak and Jestina Jones when I was a schoolboy and those later on in life like Archie Taylor Johnson, Keifala Samura, Allie Marrah, Vincent Sevallie, and Joseph Amara. My doubles partners Charles Hubbard Snr, Souad Michael, and late Colonel Max Kanga (probably the only Bo School boy who plays tennis well!)

were simply awesome at national tournaments. I recall that many good players were given the opportunity of gaining employment at Sierra Rutile. We ensured that we trained them in technical disciplines. Many like Philip Moiba, a surveyor, Sahr Nuwah, an electrician, trained at Sierra Rutile are still gainfully employed in their professions elsewhere. Many more serious players around the country like Charles Hubbard Jnr., Vincent Sevali and Edwin Michael are excelling in their professions.

Professionals, politicians and businessmen loved the game. I recollect we had well organised club teams like the Murray Town (army) club, Bo club, Mobimbi club, and Yengema club, which even played inter club tournaments at which the teams were backed by travelling support groups that included many professionals and businessmen. Former President Momoh, an ardent tennis player and fan was part of the Murray Town group before he became president and would invite us to his Spur Road residence for tennis matches when he was president. Don Young, a general manager of Sierra Rutile spearheaded the drive to make Mobimbi Tennis Club the premier tennis club in the country, employing many young tennis players and sponsoring the national tournament for years. Those were the glory days.

That was then, this is now. For now I could only reflect how far we have fallen behind in tennis. This sorry story can be told of most other sports. Tennis clubs are largely non functional, the courts are in a state of disrepair and the few players that frequent them can hardly afford to buy the necessary equipment. The national tournament is a thing of the past and the sport is dying. Resuscitating it needs the concerted effort of the Ministry of Sports, business houses and the National Tennis Association. By far the largest share of the blame goes to the ministry which concentrates in an inordinate manner on soccer. With ministerial leadership, the association can be revamped and with a responsible leadership of the association business houses can be approached for sponsorship. Time for the sports ministry to act. As for me I can only sit down and reflect with nostalgia on a sport that was very much part of my life during my younger days. I know the old rugby and cricket fogies etc. would make the same complaint. Perhaps we should start the Movement for the Resuscitation of Forgotten Sports (MfRFS)!

Ponder my thoughts.

# March 18, 2013

## AFRICELL, RADIO STATIONS AND PROTEC-TIONISM

I have followed the debate surrounding the granting of a licence to a company owned by the mobile phone company Africell. Both sides have been compelling in their rationalisation of their arguments. One side says this will kill local radio stations who would be deprived of advertisement revenue. The other side says withdrawing the licence would be tantamount to protectionism. This is a free market, they argue. Various sections of the media have taken sides but I find the arguments put forward by Philip Neville (give the devil his due) persuasive. He has made a good case about the need to protect local radio stations and has mentioned that Africell tries to do everything by itself, including providing its own music and PA system for public functions. However, I chuckled when a gentleman from a health NGO (non-governmental organization) joined the fray on the side of Africell with the justification that this was a human rights issue. My head spins! So many interest groups have joined the debate that I shudder to raise my head above the parapet lest I be pilloried. It suffices to say that after much obfuscation by Natcom (the National Telecommunications Commission) and the Independent Media Commission (IMC) in the cause of justifying their actions, I applaud the Ministry of Information calling for a temporary suspension of the licence whilst it further considers the issue, notwithstanding their initial alleged complicity.

In fairness to Africell, it has mentioned that it will continue the advertisements and other inducements it had been providing for community and commercial radio stations and intends to reflect this in a memorandum of understanding (MoU). The problem though is that the MoU may not be ironclad and may only be for a brief while. Community and commercial radio stations provide a valuable service in information dissemination that help bolster our fragile democracy. They run marginal operations at best. If other mobile phone companies or commercial companies follow in Africell's footsteps the problem could be compounded. It may however be possible for the problem to be resolved to the mutual benefit of all parties.

Engendering local participation in supplies and services should be taken seriously by various foreign-owned companies. Although the matter of stimulating community benefits is more germane to the mining industry, it applies also to other sectors. The Local Content Policy does attempt to address this issue and if experience is what we should go by, companies will not necessarily encourage local participation in their businesses voluntarily. The new policy aims to ensure a sufficient linkage between foreign enterprises and the local economy. It clarifies government's expectations of investors regarding workforce and supply chain development and sets specific performance targets. This is now the norm in many other countries.

It is becoming common in mining policies that contracts include a schedule of graduated benefits to the local community. That is, a certain percentage of employment in the mine, must go to local community members. The company should also have an obligation to provide training to local community members to make them employable. There is also often an obligation to procure an increasing percentage of a company's outsourcing from local providers, with a similar training obligation. For some operations individuals from the surrounding communities could be hired for temporary employment through 'village contracts' to provide services in property security, rehabilitation and housekeeping. Companies could also be engaged in projects to provide financial assistance to local suppliers to allow them to improve production and supply the mining company.

Many wrongly think this borders on protectionism and will not allow us to develop a competitive private sector that can hold its own in the global economy. Indeed in terms of the perceived capacity of local service providers to meet the requirements of investors, many of the local service providers are faced with financial and operating capacity issues. A gradualist approach can however be taken to address the problems of capacity limitations by a combination of training, funding and other provisions. Without the proper incentives in place, well-intentioned local supplier development initiatives can easily fail.

The figure for utilisation of local supplies in Sierra Leone is alarming for some sectors. According to a recent study, it varies from 0.1 percent in the oil and gas sector to 5.8 percent in mining and 45.6 percent in banking. There are many practical things the government can do to redress this situation. Have we ever considered why we import furniture for big government and industrial contracts when we could actively encourage local companies to set up shop? Can we not mandate that only locally produced rice may be sold to the prisons and government institutions? Can mobile phone companies not be mandated to procure certain services locally as suggested by Mr Neville? Obviously these cannot be done overnight but the Local Content Policy may allow us to roll them out gradually. Maybe — just maybe — we can learn something from this radio station imbroglio.

## THE PA SYNDROME

The term 'Pa' is so commonly used in Sierra Leone in so many different contexts that when you are called "Pa" you have to carefully examine the motive behind the bestowal of this title in order to appreciate it. Time was when Pa was venerated. It stood (and still stands in some instances) as a title for an old person, as a sign of respect. Ours has always been a society that respects and venerates people.

Pa is now so accepted nationally that it defies any tribal strictures. It is used in so many diverse situations that one has to take a closer look at the prevailing situation before appreciating it. Here are a few examples of its use:

**The respectful Pa**: This respect can either be because of the age of the conferee or his perceived status. An older driver or gardener may even call his boss 'Pa'. Of course some may be overly biased in their respect at the detriment of others. I recall a new, chauvinistic driver I had aggressively questioning my wife when she asked him to take her somewhere with my vehicle. *"You don tell the Pa eh?"* He questioned. Needless to say his employment was short-lived for this and other equally chauvinistic misdemeanours. No prizes for guessing who did the sacking.

**The derisory Pa**. Many a time those calling you pa especially "Di Pa" want something from you which they seek with flattery. *"Di pa, yu borbor day ya oh"*. In this day and age when youths think they know it all and are ably represented in various spheres of life, they could use Pa in a contemptible form. *"Den Pa den sef", "We nor want any Pa na ya, nar we compin young man we want."*

**The political Pa:** President Kabbah was amiably called Pa Kabbah. This was because of his leadership and advancement in years. This was said fondly. President Koroma has not been called Pa Koroma probably because there are so many other ways his ardent supporters may refer to him. "Di Pa" more or less confers on him the status of the ultimate authority in the country. A campaign slogan during the last presidential election was *"Di Pa dey wok"*. It soon caught on and was used by his party especially to convince the public that he was producing positive results particularly in the infrastructure area. APC (the All People's Congress political party) is probably eternally grateful for the slogans *"Di Pa dey wok"* and *"4 for 4"* which made several otherwise unpopular candidates ride on the coattails of a seemingly popular president. Ministers constantly make reference to "the Pa in his wisdom" inspiring and supporting one effort or another as if to say they themselves are totally bereft of any initiative. One even managed to place "infinite" before the wisdom. Sacrilege! On another note, I don't know if the story that made the rounds during my younger days about a bald-headed tennis player (name withheld) is true. It is said that as a partner of the then vice president, Kamara Taylor, he would pull his hair every time the Pa missed, cursing under his breath *"Dis Pa pwell!"* (And that was often), but then after making eye contact with him would say "hard luck, sir". His baldness was attributed to this perennial feat. Hapless fellow!

Despite all the adulation, our leaders are often not lulled into a false sense of security as others have been. History is replete with such examples in which rulers are given a god-like public image, often through unquestioning flattery and praise. It is said that Togo's Gnassingbé Eyadéma maintained an extensive personality cult, to the point of having schoolchildren begin their day by singing his praises. Stalin at his own instigation was often referred to as "the greatest leader", "sublime strategist of all times and nations." What modesty! We haven't gone that far yet. We just refer to ours as Di Pa.

Ponder my thoughts.

# March 26, 2014

## PUNISH NATIONAL INFRASTRUCTURE SABO-TEURS

My domestic help, a few decades back during my bachelor days, had a penchant for stealing. She would place a Maggi seasoning cube in the pot in my presence and then quickly pull it out and packet it as soon as I moved away. Talk about senseless stealing! Some people actually steal because there is something to be stolen even if the economic benefits are minuscule. Others have absolutely no respect for other people's convenience and steal anything that could make them money. Their stealing is not opportunistic but actually planned. In Sierra Leone theft or wilful damage involving national infrastructure is commonplace. The public who would readily criticise the government or a company for poor provision of infrastructural services is often loathe to condemn wilful damage or theft of such services.

Examples galore exist of theft of national infrastructure components of services. I was shocked to learn that thieves were removing the base course aggregate from the Lungi to Port Loko road being constructed and placing the stones in their backyard for beautification. Theft of electric cables and even cutting down of poles is commonplace. I recall that a major problem faced by National Power Authority (NPA) during the construction of the transmission line from Dodo to Bo and Kenema was the theft of the poles which went into the making of pots. People steal oil from NPA transformers rendering them ineffective or even causing permanent damage, thus depriving the public of electricity. Mobile phone companies with sites in remote environments experience the same problem with theft and vandalism and spend an inordinate amount of money on security and logistics to supply fuel and materials to their sites. I recall when I worked at Sierra Rutile that a case of diarrhoea in the community was later attributed to market women frying cakes in flotation oil that was stolen from the mine.

The cooks and local chemists can get quite creative usually at somebody else's expense in converting stolen products to normal everyday commodities.

A considerable amount of the theft may be for the free use of infrastructure services like electricity and water. The cutting of water pipes is much too commonplace. Usually the perpetrators may just want to extract water at that point or they may want to route new pipes to their houses. Whatever the case it results in damage to valuable infrastructure and wastage. No wonder Guma Valley Water Company loses as much as 40 percent of water pumped. Electricity theft is another matter. Bypassing of electricity meters is commonplace. Illegal abstraction of electricity can also take other forms like directly connecting from the pole to the perpetrators' houses. There is suspicion also that a lot of this is done with the acquiescence of some NPA staff.

In all of these cases, the repercussions are far reaching. The nation loses a considerable amount of money from physical damage and theft of services. Theft can also be dangerous and lead to accidents or even death. Electricity bypassing may be dangerous not only to the perpetrators but to the public. Depriving crucial emergency facilities of electricity or remote communities of mobile phone facilities could also be life threatening.

These problems are not unusual in Africa, but a lot of countries are addressing them through well implemented legislation. Wanton destruction of telecommunication support systems in particular has become a major cause for concern in Africa. The insurgent group, Boko Haram, bombed 25 masts in the north-eastern part of Nigeria recently. This forced the Nigerian government to re-think its policy on safeguarding ICT infrastructure. The Nigerian federal government collaborated with the Nigerian Communications Commission (NCC) and the private telecommunications operators to come up with an ICT infrastructure protection bill. Damage to fibre cables resulting from road construction and maintenance, indiscriminate vandalism of cables and other network infrastructure results in over 60 percent of major breakdowns in telecoms infrastructure in some countries. A report from Uganda indicates that losses incurred involved $1.533 million due to cuts and theft of fibre optic cables, while $2.918 million was spent on maintaining and repairing the damages. Some people in Tanzania have been excavating the fibre optic cables because they think it is copper wire that could be sold to scrap metal dealers

In Kenya the Energy and Communications Law (Amendment) Act 2011 increased the penalties of those caught in unsavoury acts to a fine of $58,000 and a jail term of no less than 10 years. Previously offenders could walk away with a $1,164 fine or three years imprisonment. There is also provision in the law that acts as a deterrent to the practice where contractors and utility firms dig up cable without regard for existing underground infrastructure.

A cogent poser in Sierra Leone should therefore be whether or not state infrastructure should be classed as critical infrastructure or services classed as critical whose illegal abstraction would be regarded as economic sabotage. The new Electricity Act has provision for penalties for electricity theft but this is neither well defined nor stiff and the law has not been made to bite. Time for a general law to cover all critical national infrastructure!

## CUSTOMER SERVICE: THE BANE OF SIERRA LEONEAN BUSINESSES

One of the things people hate about going to business houses is the disproportionate amount of time spent there and the shoddy treatment. Customer care should be done right. As one writer says it's a business thing. In Sierra Leone, for many, time is very much still a relative concept. For businesses to grow there needs to be structure and punctuality. There also needs to be a high sense of accountability.

Some of you may have had similar experiences to mine at one time or another. You are sitting in a restaurant waiting to place a further order and the three waitresses are all watching football totally oblivious of your presence until you shout. I once went to a restaurant in Bo with a friend and we both ordered chicken. After some 45 minutes, a lady walked in with a couple of live chicken in her hand. "Nah now yu dey cam? the waitress asked. We got up and walked out. In restaurants and pubs it often takes ages for your bill to be prepared. And the odd pint or two would probably be added to your bill if you are not attentive. For a particular barmaid in my normal watering hole, it was a case of mathematics gone awry. A bill of much less than Le100,000 turned out to be several million Leones. On checking the mathematically challenged ex Harfordian (yes, she had impressed us earlier with stories of her academic prowess at Harford) had lined up her figures in the wrong columns and was making vein attempts at defending her addition.

Members of a work team I sent out recently to a major town in Kailahun (name withheld to protect the dignity of my district) were thrilled that the hotel proprietor could offer them self - contained rooms. On finding out there were no toilets in the rooms or indeed the house, they queried "It is self-contained?"

"Everything is contained in the compound including the toilet, "he said, pointing to a pit latrine at the back of the house. I will leave mobile phone companies out of this discussion as whatever excuses they give may give may not be worth the paper they are written on. I must say however that whatever customer service problems there may be with banks, they are now much better at serving customers, now that you have a proliferation of them. A few years back, terse treatment of customers at the few major Banks was much too commonplace. We could learn a lot from

Lebanese traders who would often treat you like royalty especially if you are a valued customer. They go to great lengths to please the buyer. An old story that made the rounds some time ago was of a Lebanese trader who was asked if he had carbon dioxide. "A nor get tam now but ar go get am next week" was his reply.

It is the responsibility of managers to ensure that the relevant soft skills are available by either recruiting polite and friendly staff or by ensuring that existing or new staff are trained. Also the right environment should be created to influence the attitude of staff. However, it is one thing getting trained and quite another following things up in the field. The problem may be partly cultural. Time also does not mean much to a lot of employees and they may not even have any performance criteria against which they are judged. Whatever the case some of it is just plain bad manners. Perhaps it is high time for us to have an independent customer complaints radio programme to complement the work done by existing groups and give awards to high performing institutions and publicise them. Customer charters that set out standards for major factors important to the customer with penalty clauses should be encouraged by regulators. Customers should be made to be loyal for business to thrive. We should remember the long-established fact that it costs about five times as much to acquire a new customer than it does to keep an existing one.

Ponder my thoughts.

# April 2, 2013

## PRESIDENT KOROMA'S US VISIT: WHAT OBAMA DID NOT SAY

I had an uncle who always used to impress us with his academic prowess. "When I came first in class, no one came second or third. The next student would be given fourth position because of the vast difference in our exam marks." Why do I retell this story of self praise? I will come back to that later.

By all accounts, President Koroma's visit to President Obama in the company of three other African presidents has been very successful. The accolades paid to the country and the president would be extremely pleasing to any well-meaning Sierra Leonean.

President Obama in his statement to the press talked about stability, elections, governance, accountability and economic development:

"Sierra Leone just 10 years ago was in the midst of as brutal a civil war as we've ever seen. And yet, now we've seen consecutive fair and free elections. And under President Koroma's leadership, we've seen not only good governance, but also significant economic growth...When you have democracies that work, sound management of public funds, transparency and accountability to the citizens that put leaders in place — that is not only good for the state and the functioning of government, it's also good for economic development because it gives people confidence, it attracts business, it facilitates trade and commerce."

Human capacity building, education and youth issues also featured in Obama's statement:

"...And that means building human capacity and improving education and job skills for rapidly growing and young populations...and individuals like President Koroma have taken great interest in finding additional ways that we can recruit and engage young people not only to get involved in public service but also to get involved in entrepreneurship that helps build these countries."

Conflict puts paid to economic development, added Obama: "Obviously, economic development, prosperity doesn't happen if you have constant conflict...Some like President Koroma has seen that firsthand."

According to President Obama, the infiltration of terrorism into the region and drug cartels that are using West Africa in particular as a transit point also undermines some of the progress that's been made.

Congratulations Mr President for bringing recognition to Sierra Leone! As one keen observer of the political scene put it; "Even if these ascriptions are not totally accurate, it's a starter and this cocktail of recognition clearly insulated the national pride in me. My only wish is that this international goodwill translates into tangible evidence of economic progress on the ground. As a Sierra Leonean, I wish the[e] president well. Because we can only be a better nation if this president is a better President."

When the trip is done and dusted and President Koroma returns to Sierra Leone, he will encounter on a daily basis extreme challenges in the very areas for which he was lauded by President Obama.

Obama talked about capacity building stressing the need for education and skills training for youths. The situation on the ground if far from being rosy. The tenuous state of the universities with their constant strikes, teacher employment and certification and the myriad problems of the education sector should gall anyone interested in education. The prognosis does not look good and the budget allocation to sort out the problem is woefully inadequate. Only Le 775 million will be spent on technical vocational education out of Le 133.9 billion on education in the 2013 budget. Most of the money allocated to the youth and sports sector is allocated to international sports organisation. Very little money seems to be spent in addressing the youth unemployment problem, especially with 800,000 unemployed youths.

In the area of transparency and accountability, the latest Auditor General's report and the Extractive Industries Transparency Initiative (EITI) debacle do not do us proud. There is need to take transparency and accountability in the use of public finds more seriously.

The praise for the considerable strides made in the area of governance should be shared with others. As another keen observer has noted, "the SLPP played a major role in sustaining the "democratic trajectory" in Sierra Leone by ending the war, holding 3 consecutive peaceful elections, and handing over power peacefully in the third. " I am certain the President recognises and appreciates this. Statements like the one made by Ex Ambassador John Leigh in which he did not recognise the efforts of President Koroma's predecessor could prove divisive. John Leigh said:"President Osama recognizes that of the four honouree presidents, President Koroma came the longest way and most difficult route...the other presidents sprang up from bases created by their predecessors whereas EBK (Ernest Bai Koroma) is creating a solid foundation for future SL leaders to build upon."

I can only refer John Leigh to my "clever" uncle. Other people need to be praised once in a while.

Sierra Leone has witnessed frenetic activities in the business sector lately. As an investment destination, new businesses are springing up every day and we have moved up significantly in the "Doing Business Index". This however needs to be translated into greater opportunities for Sierra Leonean entrepreneurs. The president should also be mindful of the fact that business initiatives are still being stalled because of extremely high interest rates. Competition may also be stifled by unfair procurement practices.

Some have questioned the USA's motive as being more for addressing the problems of terrorism and drug smuggling from a sub-regional perspective than anything else. True that President Koroma also had a meeting with US Secretary of Defence Hagel to discuss cooperation on shared regional security and peacekeeping in Africa. Whatever the objectives, one cannot dispute the fact that good governance, security, capacity building and all the problems mentioned by President Obama are good for our country. Whatever our political proclivity, the government should be supported in any initiatives to address these. We should however not only be swift to bless but also swift to chide. The president can act on the tremendous international goodwill he is getting and work sincerely on our intractable problems.

Congratulations Mr President, but...

## OUR GRADUATES: SO YOU CAN'T READ, WRITE, OR SPEAK ENGLISH?

The story is told of a man who went on a business trip with his girlfriend and decided to send a text message to his wife: "I wish you were her", he texted. He ended up with a broken skull when he got back home for leaving the "e" out of "here". Beware of spellings! They could tell the truth.

If you are like me you must have worked with countless graduates over the years. My greatest disappointment is that many cannot read, write or speak English. Whatever your job your objective presentation of facts in a report will be used to assist in decision making. This could range from a simple one-pager to a several hundred page feasibility study, investigative report, progress report, trip report, or more. Reports must be skilfully planned, logically sequenced, objective, accurate, reliable, and easy to read. Unfortunately our graduates frequently find reports challenging to write and structure appropriately. They also find it difficult to write proposals.

Many graduates cannot even write application letters well and their resumes are filled with glaring spelling mistakes. I recall the story of a manager at a parastatal I worked for on contract, who would always blame his secretary when some spelling mistakes or incomplete sentences appeared in his reports. "Dis gal fool", he would tell me in vexation. When this got to the secretary's ear she secretly went to my office, got out the original manuscript and announced with glee "Nar in write am, Sir. Dis man pas mak".

After several attempts to get a final year engineering student to explain some dubious aspects of his project to us on the examining panel, the dean, an irreverent friend of mine, asked him 'Can you explain that to us in Mende?'

Perhaps the biggest assassin of the English language was a supervisor at Nitti in Sierra Rutile who would always address his American manager, Chris as "Christ". "Dear Christ, the conveyor has turnobored". . Chris in exasperation would protest-"This guy thinks I am divine".

I sometimes wonder if some read anything at all after college. I was once involved in a job interview for an environmentalist.

"What do you mean by climate change? I asked.

"Well in Sierra Leone there are two seasons-the rainy season and the dry season. The climate changes between these two seasons." I held back on the next question on the definition of sustainable development.

Public speaking or indeed even normal conversation in English can also be a challenge.

There is no doubt that our colleges pay scant attention to writing and presentation skills. To be fair, the problems may even emanate from the schools which do not teach students the rudimentary English required to cope with work. Simple tenses become a challenge. The colleges could contemplate arranging classes in report writing and requiring them to make public presentations. They should also be trained to be more research oriented. There are also many such courses now run by the Institute of Public Administration and Management (IPAM) in which they can be enrolled.

To be fair, not all graduates are that bad. In case workers I am currently associated with are reading this, I am referring to former employees in this article!

Ponder my thoughts.

# April 8, 2013

## THE CONUNDRUM OF THE CONSTITUTION

The airwaves have been inundated with programmes more recently on the proposed Constitutional Review process. Several bodies have expressed their opinions on what changes are required.

A constitution is the basic law or laws of a nation or a state, which sets out how that state will be organized by deciding the powers and authorities of government between different political units, and by stating the basic law-making and structural principles of society.

Apart from the fundamental obligations of government and the various objectives - political, social, economic, foreign policy — recognition and protection of fundamental human rights and freedoms of the individuals as well as issues of finance, it could delve into a whole range of affairs of state.

I will attempt to veer away from the "legalese" and get right down to brass tacks by asking the question: What is wrong that we are trying to change? My comments are not exhaustive but rather based on what I consider to be some of the most important issues to consider. I will however dwell inordinately on economic empowerment.

**The Wheels of Justice:** Despite the improvements made in the judiciary there are a considerable number of challenges which could bring about unnecessary unrest. The independence of the judiciary is questioned when the executive branch has an inordinate say in the appointment and tenure of judges. The electoral cases still pending for Constituencies 5 and 15 that have been left bereft of parliamentary representatives, and the delay in the electoral case before the Supreme Court being pursued by the opposition, are symptomatic of the slow turning of the wheels of justice dealing with representation of the people. Some may argue that this could happen whichever party is in power. That is really beside the point. Whatever the case such happenings are inimical to proper representation and national reconciliation. We have however seen from the recent Kenyan example that such issues can be speedily addressed.

**Private sector development:** The constitution may refer to economic freedom, equal opportunities and all the buzzwords that would engender the growth of the private sector. There are however several things that can thwart this if not addressed in government accountability structures. The role of parliament in approving agreements, the structure and limits imposed on devolved units etc. would inhibit the private sector.

**Women representatives**: This has been discussed for so long that it is high time this issue is treated seriously. Other countries have addressed it in a more tangible way. In the Kenyan constitution, representation in elective bodies has to effectively meet a gender equity constitutional requirement, namely that no more than two-thirds of members shall be from either gender in its makeup. A women's representative Member of Parliament (MP) is elected from each county, therefore guaranteeing a minimum of 47 women MPs in the National Assembly.

**Politics of Exclusion and Taking Economic Power to the local level**: A lot of things come into play here. These include ethnicity, structure of government etc. It is well known that the decentralization process has not worked well and actual power rests with central government, which controls the purse strings. The devolution of functions also leaves a lot to be desired. Only 58 out of the total of 72 functions slated for devolution have been devolved to Local Councils. Many local councils as well as chiefdom councils have failed to deliver on their mandates for efficient service delivery to communities while the authority of paramount chiefs is often undermined for partisan considerations.

Many political observers are of the view that our democratic system based on "majoritarianism" which divides people arithmetically into a majority and a minority and states that the minority must yield to the majority is not part of African culture. In a society like ours where parties are mainly formed along tribal and regional lines this may either lead to the politics of exclusion or the politics of acquiescence. Whatever the case, this does not bode well for the development of the country as the success of the system depends too much on the whims of those in power. The state becomes dominated by the party in power. Public resources and public property are placed in the service of the party in power, which, in most cases, is the majority party.

A respected governance expert, Dele Jones, refers to the need for addressing the ethnic problems we face in Sierra Leone and suggests a con-federal system that takes power away from the center to geographical units. Research seems to suggest that peoples' need for identity, security, recognition, participation, and autonomy is of paramount importance and that conflict is inevitable in any society where people are denied their basic needs for identity, equality, recognition, security, dignity and participation. Conflict is more likely to be managed in a country with reasonable economic growth. Jones says there is little economic empowerment if power is kept at the center in a situation like ours in which you have a multiplicity of ethnic groups. Some other experts agree but say we should not go as far as accepting the Swiss model which he touts. Most however agree that decentralization and devolution must be enhanced. The sorry state of Kono, where most of the diamonds in Sierra Leone have been produced since 1935 should really compel us to take a harder look at the inequities and gross unfairness in distribution of economic resources.

I know everyone and his dog will have something to say about the Constitution soon. The final document would need to be backed by necessary pieces of legislation, putting in the necessary structures and having checks and balances in place. Above all there must be the political will to "do the right thing". Some countries like England and New Zealand do not even have written constitutions. They depend on time-honored customs and conventions and of course a good judiciary. Our constitution must however be adapted to an evolving state with peculiar challenges. It must be adapted to the various crises of human affairs which we face.

A note of caution however is in place. It is undoubtedly not going to be an easy process and there will be many who will clamour for their own interests or even some who will try to thwart it for various reasons. After all Niccolo Machiavelli in his 1611 book, The Prince, warned:

"There is nothing more difficult to arrange, more doubtful of success, and more dangerous to carry through than initiating change in a State's constitution. The innovator makes enemies of all those who prospered under the old order, and only lukewarm support is forthcoming from those who could prosper under the new. Their support is lukewarm partly from fear of their adversaries, who have the existing law on their side, and partly because men are generally incredulous, never really trusting new things unless they have tested them by experience."

## THE GRASSROOTS SHOULD NOT BE FED GRASS

I recall the true story of someone in Bo who wanted to be a political supporter of mine. "Mr. Keili," he said. "I have listened to you a lot and although I went to Bo school, I am a big fan of yours. I have formed a grassroots movement for you in Bo. When are you coming so we can embezzle together over some drinks?" After an incredulous gasp at the thought of "embezzling", I answered politely that I would not be coming to Bo soon. Oh this grassroots business!

The keen observer will note that our politics has been overshadowed by the nebulous? group known as grassroots. Ignore them at your peril! Grassroots movements usually have aims of self preservation.

A grassroots movement is often driven by the politics of a community. Grassroots movements are often at the local level, as many volunteers in the community give their time to support the local party, which can lead to helping the national party. By its very nature, it is fiercely resistant to central control — yet it can be incomparably loyal and self-sacrificing. Properly understood and respected (and hence properly utilized), it has the potential to alter an entire culture. Approached incorrectly, it will turn on those who seek to exploit it.

There is no doubt that grassroots pressure causes a government or any political party to think twice about various issues. This is not necessarily a bad thing as it defines the aspirations of the people. Regrettably however, the spectre of extortion, violence and lawlessness now seems to mar the performance of our grassroots movements. The street trader who refuses to move his wares from the street, an okada rider who believes he should not keep to the rules, and Ataya base members who would want to build their "bases" anywhere are often not confronted with honesty because of the fear of losing votes. Politicians muster troops of ill-disciplined youths who harass opponents whilst their conniving cohorts tell party members: "listen to the voice of the grassroots". Let's face it, anyone with some cash to buy food and booze and some loose change to give to these youths could muster "grassroots support".

Should we not really be asking ourselves the question whether we are educating the grassroots. Have we not compromised too much? Are we feeding the grassroots "grass" for our own selfish motives? Let us be reminded of the words of James Lowell when he says "Compromise makes a good umbrella, but a poor roof".

The grassroots should not be fed grass.

Ponder my thoughts.

# April 16, 2013

## UMARU FOFANA: THE DAWN LEADS ON AN-OTHER DAY FOR SLAJ

Whether or not you know Umaru Fofana you cannot help but be impressed by his imprints on the Sierra Leone Association of Journalists (SLAJ). There was a time when the journalistic profession was looked at locally with derision. During Umaru's reign however when SLAJ speaks you sit up and listen.

Here are a few admirable qualities Umaru has displayed in his leadership of SLAJ:

**Consistency and respect for the law:** Like him or not, he has been consistent. His views on many issues indicate he is immutable unless when faced with changing circumstances. His views on the Sierra Leone Broadcasting Corporation (SLBC) issue for example have not changed. He is a great respecter of the law and laid down structures. His views on the closure of the two political radio stations, which he is against have been quite unequivocal.

**Courage:** Umaru has been vociferous on many occasions in defence of journalists. This has often placed him in the crosshairs of senior government functionaries including ministers. I have heard him make tough but not irreverent remarks at least on two occasions when responding to comments made by government Ministers. When he thinks condemnation for some lapse on the government's part should probably come right from the president, he has said so. He however does this with due deference even though he would be ready to stand his ground when he suspects bully tactics.

**Vision:** His vision for the establishment is in realisation of the fact that SLAJ's problems are numerous and cannot be solved overnight. He set himself an ambitious target and has admittedly had short shrift on some of these issues. These include the Freedom of Information (FOI) bill and the SLAJ headquarters. He is however quick to admit that he encountered problems but would be supportive of any actions by his successor to address them.

**Pragmatism**: I have crossed swords with him over his defence of the rights and conditions of work for journalists. That he could do this without being offensive is a measure of the man's stature. He tells you as it is and advocates passionately for them. He is however understanding of the immense problems faced by newspaper proprietors and comes out looking tough, but understanding and practical with a bent for sorting out the problem rather than engaging in needless rancour.

**Integrity**: In his BBC reports, he is the quintessential journalist seeking the truth in an ethical manner. Even under pressure, Umaru has not buckled to practising gutter journalism. He gives as good as he gets but does not lose his cool. His integrity has also extended to the management of SLAJ's financial resources. I have not asked Umaru about his political proclivity. Whatever it is, his consistency is hallmarked by the fact that some in the SLPP used to consider him as APC and others in APC now consider him as SLPP. I have not known him to sacrifice his professional integrity because of this.

**Selflessness:** Stories abound of his selfless defence of journalists who have been physically attacked or unfairly incarcerated. Umaru has been known for visiting police stations at midnight. That he has used his own resources often for SLAJ related business is common knowledge.

SLAJ has taken a consistent position on national issues deserving of its intervention. No one now treats SLAJ with a sleight of the hand despite the failings of its individual members.

There are a lot of success stories in journalism. Some newspapers despite all the difficulties have raised the standards of newspapers to a new high-with well sourced stories on various spheres of life.

The journalism profession has however been bedevilled by several challenges. Though the Mass Communications Department at Fourah Bay College (FBC) and other programmes may be doing their bit to train journalists with a fair measure of success, standards are still very low. Press freedom should not however mean unsustainable business practices Many press houses face economic challenges. Newspapers cannot survive on sales which do not even cover operating costs. Advertisement revenues from a comparatively small market have got to be shared among some forty something newspapers. The top newspapers are only kept afloat because they earn revenue from peripheral income sources associated with their business like printing. For the electronic press, advertisement revenues are low. The reality however is that there are far too many newspapers.

Having more exacting standards to qualify for opening up a newspaper may however mean fewer newspapers and less people in the profession, which in my view will not be a bad thing. SLAJ would not admit it, but somehow, this issue of unsustainable practices has to be addressed.

Umaru has shown that SLAJ can play a yeoman's role in maintaining journalistic standards and ethics. Public enlightenment is the forerunner of justice and the foundation of democracy. It is the duty of the journalist to seek the truth and provide a comprehensive account of events and issues, striving to serve with thoroughness and honesty and maintaining good professional integrity. It behoves journalists to support the open exchange of views, even views they find repugnant. Umaru has shown that there is still hope for SLAJ to spur our journalists to embark on a path to achieve these lofty ideals. He has shown that the organisation and the profession can be respected and that you can gain national respect if you bring respect to your profession.

He will be a hard act to follow. Good luck to him and his successor Kelvin Lewis

## MAN "LIVE" BY MAN

"You, out! You also, get out of here!" At this order from a security guard, to two well-dressed gentlemen waiting outside St. Anthony's Church hall to join the after funeral repast of a friend's father, the gentlemen walked out of the compound without so much as a mild protest. My friends and I who witnessed this bizarre episode were shocked that the guard would behave this way to mourners but were surprised at the lack of protestation from the  gentlemen.
"Pa, den man den don pasmark. Den day ya for all berin" he explained to us.

Incidences like this are much too commonplace now. Well dressed crooks now frequent all kinds of ceremonies to look for "booty". Some may attend purely for a square meal.

I recently attended a funeral service in Bo and heard someone remark at the repast that people were going to have a field day as there were three funeral services on that day. True to the prediction, a mourner walked into the repast room with a black plastic bag containing his food packet from another funeral repast. He walked up gingerly with his hymn sheet and pin-up from another service and helped himself to some more food.

The story is told of a visiting expatriate lady who went to a church that she usually attends when she is in Sierra Leone. She was followed unsuspectingly by four "worshippers" who walked off with her bag when she went for communion. Lots of ladies now go for communion with their bags clutched in their hands, giving a new meaning to the famous invitation "...Draw near with faith..." which should probably be rephrased " If you have made sure you have taken all your belongings with you and no thief will make off with your valuables, draw near with faith and receive...." The announcement in churches about making sure your valuables are collected at the end of a church service is now the norm. Just about the only thing you will be likely to recover if you leave it in church will be a bible. You cannot however be sure about this if the bible looks fairly new. I however have a philosophical view of the theft of bibles. If the thief or someone he sells it to uses it, he may be along the path of fulfilling the objectives of the "Great Commission" even if the thief flouts the eighth commandment.

Priests and families have got quite innovative at addressing these issues however. Many churches now devise contraptions by which money goes in one way and does not exit. My Dad modified the church collection bag specifically for Mammy Johnson (not her real name) who was in the habit of dropping in one thousand Leones and collecting her change of five thousand Leones. Her attendance rate dropped after the change!

I went to a funeral last year at which the priest announced at the end of the service "Announcements will be made after the interment at the cemetery". Some shady looking characters behind me immediately disappeared — the uncertainty would obviously be too much for them. Even graves are not spared. Nowadays, families usually wait till the grave is sealed before leaving the cemetery.

Many genuine and non genuine guests attend wedding receptions with their plastic bags to make off with food and drinks. When they notice gate crashers some families resort to serving by "recognition". I once went to a wedding at which I was sidestepped for food and drinks services because the servers did not "recognise" me. After several embarrassing service episodes, I made my way quietly out of the hall.

Criminals are taking advantage of our religious and social events. Some may however be looking only for a square meal. Indeed man "live" by man.

Ponder my thoughts.

# April 23, 2013

## CIVIL SOCIETY: WHEN THE HUNTER BECOMES THE HUNTED

Civil society organisations (CSOs) have become important actors for delivery of social services and implementation of other development programs, as a complement to government. Globally CSOs have influenced the shaping of public policy over the past two decades. On the local scene CSOs have been very dynamic and advocated for many issues pertinent to our national life especially since the end of the war. It is therefore surprising that they seem to be accusing each other now of not being true to the cause.

In a recent newspaper report titled "NMJD slams civil society organisations", the writer states that the group Network Movement for Justice and Development (NMJD) has criticised some CSOs in a recent report for "compromising the intents for which they are established". Referencing NMJD's report on the project titled "Initiative to Build Social Movement in Sierra Leone"; NMJD Executive Director Abu Brima lamented the lack of visionary and dynamic leadership in civil society movements accusing two civil society groups, the National Youth Coalition (NYC) and Civil Society Alternative Process (CSAP), for compromising their platforms. According to the report, "the NYC went beyond its mandate which is to advocate for the Sierra Leonean youth to taking sides on issues that have nothing to do with youth. For example the procurement of arms and ammunition by the government in which it supported the government." Brima also accused CSAP of being undemocratic and of not changing its leadership since its formation in 2004. Alternative Process's national coordinator refused to be replaced and when forced to do so had taken away sensitive documents with him. Such actions, Brima claimed, had discouraged donors from working with the organisation.

This is indeed disappointing news. No one can dispute that various types of pressure from CSOs have made government reconsider a considerable number of its policies. I have had a long association with CSOs in the extractives and environmental sectors and have been impressed with what they have done. NMJD, by far the most vociferous of the local NGOs dealing with the mining sector, has been singularly effective in bringing to the national and international media and international organisations the inequities in the sector and the perceived excesses of mining companies. Several international initiatives — such as the Kimberley Process have been spawned from the issues emanating from "conflict diamonds" and other issues related to social and economic benefits from natural resources exploitation, which have been brought to the fore by international NGOs such as Partnership Africa Canada (PAC). The role of the National Advocacy Coalition on Extractives (NACE) in educating the public about pitfalls with extractives sector agreements is well appreciated. Green Scenery has almost singlehandedly brought the issue of land grabbing to the fore. In the area of governance, Campaign for Good Governance (CGG) has been instrumental in making the public aware of concerns about governance issues. Groups like National Election Watch (NEW) have done impressive work in Sierra Leone and the sub region.

It is disconcerting that over the past few years, CSOs have appeared to be for hire. Indeed Abu Brima is right. I have mentioned the story before in this column of one gentleman from a health related NGO poking his nose into the Africell radio saga because he thought "it is a human rights issue". NMJD itself has attracted the ire of other NGOs for criticising the African Minerals agreement. Another NGO opined thus:

"The NMJD and its Executive Director, we are inclined to believe are either blind to the reality on the ground with regard the monumental developments taking place in Sierra Leone because of African Minerals, or the NMJD and its Executive Director are trouble-makers with ulterior motives."

There is little doubt that some CSOs are for hire. We have witnessed heads of CSOs condemning government on key issues, only for them to markedly shift position and be "compensated" with government appointments. It is not however the venture into politics that I find repulsive. After all, there are several examples worldwide of successful CSO members doing so. Former Brazilian president Lula da Silva was a union leader and so is the president of Venezuela, Nicolas Maduro. Bernard Kouchner, the co-founder of Médecins Sans Frontières (MSF) was later a successful French foreign minister. Back home, Alpha Timbo, ex secretary general of the Sierra Leone Teacher's Union became a successful minister. It becomes repulsive however when civil society advocates sell out the very ideals on which their organisation was founded as a condition precedent for being "invited" to serve.

CSOs can certainly contribute a lot to bolstering the work of our transparency and accountability agencies and groups. This role and other roles played by various CSOs would require training of staff, which is a necessity for many employees of CSOs. Whatever their deficiencies CSOs are good for our nascent democracy and should be encouraged. That is why we ought to applaud the sort of censorship advocated by NMJD. The adoption of undemocratic practices and unprincipled positions on issues have no place in civil society organisations. Government and corporate groups should not be seen to engender a split in their ranks for their selfish benefit. Meanwhile, it is good that they now contemplate better coordination and some form of self censorship. The question of "Quis custodiet ipsos custodes?"-"Who will guard the guards themselves?" becomes more pertinent now than ever before. Civil society can go a long way toward guarding itself.

## DOMESTIC LABOUR: THEY WHO TREAD THE PATH OF LABOUR...

I was very impressed by a presentation on Radio Democracy by Alita Ansu Katta on an indigenous business she had set up to cater for the provision of domestic and office staff for various clients. Anita was the winner of the "Business Bomba" competition and was using her prize money of Le100 million to implement her business idea.

Anita is right that training is absolutely essential. I recall the case of a houseboy of a friend at Sierra Rutile during our bachelor days. We were impressed that our friend's chairs, unlike ours, were always shiny and wanted a few tips. "Lakayana", as we fondly called the houseboy, "what is your secret to these shiny chairs?" "Ar de rub pamail pan am sir! Palm oil? So this was the source of the troublesome red stains we often had on our clothes?

Our employment figures indicate that some 80 percent of the urban and rural labour force may be underutilised. Anita's agency registers and trains staff for various domestic and office chores. She negotiates wages for them and brings them into the formal sector by registering them with the National Social Security and Insurance Trust (Nassit). She also takes out employers insurance. She stresses the need for some literacy training for some jobs. Her biggest worry, she says, is the unreliability of people and that big T word for most Sierra Leoneans -TRUST. The driver who picks up passengers and siphons fuel, the housekeeper who steals your valuables and carts away food, the cleaner who cleans out a lot more things from your house than garbage are much too commonplace now. Those of us who are much older remember with fondness some housekeeper or driver we had when we were kids. Not anymore.

Put up your hands if you could employ a driver if you found one that was honest. Your hands up again, if you allow a domestic worker to clean the rooms in your absence. How many of you allow the houseboy to measure rice or take condiments from the store in your absence? Many people do not bother employing staff for domestic chores as they cannot stand the frustration. Busy housewives now double as maids, cleaners and drivers.

I have always been impressed with domestic staff in Ghana during my visits there, and many friends can attest to their relative reliability compared to Sierra Leonean domestic staff. We should honestly ask ourselves: Are Ghanaians more honest than we are? Is the lack of trust now imprinted on our collective national psyche? We must take action to engender trust between employer and employee — but how do we start doing this? Is this one big homework for the ABC Secretariat to handle? In Ghana you could go to an employment agency and get a well recommended domestic worker and you can almost be certain the recommendation is authentic. As far as Sierra Leone is concerned Alita has entered into uncharted territory which is nevertheless useful in addressing our employment problems. We could potentially create considerably more jobs than we care to admit.

The ILO's Decent Work Agenda provides a new and promising avenue for ensuring visibility and respect for domestic workers. Other countries have enshrined this issue into their labour laws. Oh, I almost forgot. Is the perception that many Sierra Leoneans don't want to earn an honest wage true? Sierra Leonean workers should realise there is dignity in labour and God looks favourably on honest labour. As the hymn writer says:

They who tread the path of labour follow where my feet have trod; they who work without complaining, do the holy will of God; nevermore thou needest seek me; I am with thee everywhere; raise the stone, and thou shalt find me, cleave the wood and I am there.
Good luck to Alita.
Ponder my thoughts.

# April 30, 2013

## 52 YEARS OF INDEPENDENCE: THE TIMES THEY ARE A-CHANGIN'

The times they are a-changin'. Fifty years ago, I could flip the electricity switch and the room would immediately be lit. Now more often than not I turn them on only when that noisy thing called a generator is on. Fifty years ago, I could open the tap and drink clean water. Today, even when I could afford it, I spend my time chasing Guma to supply water to my tank. Forty something years ago, there were less than 30 students with me in class at CKC. The teachers were devoted and well paid. Today the teacher has lost all respect and dignity and many teachers are now tagged as "ghosts". They don't show up? Our schools are bursting at the seams and the only way we can cope is to have a shift system. Some forty-something years ago the railway was in its heyday and rural farmers could take their crops to the cities. Today this is a thing of the past. Okay I can go on and on! The fact remains that our living standards have fallen constantly since independence in 1961.

As a nation, the euphoria of independence was overtaken by a realisation that we did not have a solid pervasive foundation in governance, education or infrastructure on which to anchor our nascent state firmly and embark upon a path of sustainable development. Our educational system had been geared towards training administrators. The number of doctors, engineers and middle level technical people was pitifully low. A prolonged period of one party governance, a series of coups and a rebel war that devastated our economy have all come and gone.

Post war, we have rebuilt, rehabilitated, tinkered with governance structures, embarked on a sustained period of democracy and are hopefully on a path of change and prosperity.

I would hate to wallow in pity. Let's however take a reality check. The real problems with our actions have been the absence of sustainable practices in the face of socio-economic challenges, a growing population (from 2.3 million in 1961 to 5.6 million now) as well as external challenges. Our economy has always been largely based on natural resources. This situation has not changed much. Also, since the sixties, some 60 percent of our rural folk have been in subsistence agriculture. That has not changed much. It is little wonder that we have a 70 percent poverty rate.

There are obviously a lot this and previous governments have attempted to do to redress the situation. Suffice it to say however that many actions are still ephemeral. Fifty-two years after independence we should really adopt a paradigm shift from the way we have been doing business. I will not attempt to suggest concrete solutions but would rather dwell a bit on some of the underlying problems that still need to be addressed.

We cannot develop as a nation if we do not have national cohesion. This and previous governments have tried to tinker with the system but there are some underlying problems which would have to be addressed. A nation is characterised as integrated if it meets the following requirements:

1. There is a significant numerical representation of each component group in the institutions of the nation

2. Such groups are distributed throughout the institutional structures of the nation

3. Each group enjoys equality and power within the nation and its institutions

4. All areas of the country enjoy equitable and balanced development.

The "state vehicle" is used to take us on the "development" journey. Let us examine ourselves to see how far we have come since independence. Politicians still continue to use the instruments of the state to enrich themselves and their cronies. Our democratic system is based on "majoritarialism" and parties are mainly formed along tribal and regional lines. Our system of governance is such that the state is always dominated by the party in power.

We must address the many problems thwarting the growth of the private sector. Access to capital, legal impediments, bureaucracy, and poor infrastructure services will continue to thwart the private sector unless they are seriously addressed. Successive governments have mainly paid lip service to the growth of the private sector and despite their rhetoric the formal private sector is still very small.

We should also realise that if we do not address our education and skills training problems seriously we will always be in the doldrums. Human capacity building is a common thread that affects the operation of various sectors of our economy. It is important that technical skills are provided for youths in areas relevant for the Sierra Leonean job market. We must diversify the economy and gear ourselves toward a knowledge economy.

Admittedly there are a lot of good things planned on paper. To translate all of these into reality would need political will. I dare say that political will largely comes from the government in power but the opposition should also play its part.

We must not however despair. Certain things have changed. The services sector of the economy has grown with banks, hotels and all kinds of services. Some aspects of infrastructure to a certain degree have imporoved - telecoms for example. Some more mines have reopened so we can have a second bite at the cherry. Sierra Leoneans in the diaspora are ready to help with a renewed vigour All is not lost Mama Salone!

A good 52 years after independence, we Sierra Leoneans should recognise that personal sacrifice on our part is essential. This nation was built by great and famous men who made personal sacrifices. Let us remember them in words of the hymn "Now praise ye great and famous men"

*Praise we the wise and brave and strong,*
*Who graced their generation,*
*Who helped the right, and fought the wrong,*
*And made our folk a nation.*

## INDEPENDENCE AWARDS: THIS LADY IS NOT FOR TURNING

*Has not the potter power over the clay, of the same lump to make one vessel of honor, and another to dishonor?-Romans 9:21*

It is heartening that whilst we have all our problems to grapple with after 52 years of independece, we could take time off to honor those to whom honor is due. I was pleased to see my old mining engineer friend Alpha Kanu and my old neighbour Dr. Sam Sesay. Together with professors Victor Strasser King, Jonas Redwood Sawyerr and Abu Sesay they had received the highest accolade-Commander of the Order of the Republic of Sierra Leone (CRSL). The three professors had contributed so much to higher education, administration and policy issues in Sierra Leone. The honorees were from various spheres of life. Sahr Wonday had an award for services to the mining sector. Sahr with over forty years of experience in the mining industry now heads the new National Minerals Agency. Andrina Coker, our deputy Bank of Sierra Leone governor was honoured for her significant work in the central bank. Donald Osman had done a lot of philanthropic work in giving assistance to hospitals through his organisation, Lead Global Inc.. Hawa Turay Sesay had done a lot in  philantrophic work in the education arena-building and operating schools. Odette Awada -who does not know Mammy Awada in Bo? For over fifty years she has run her educational institutions in B. Her award is long overdue. Dr James Caisa Boima's work in medicine is legendary. One of the best surgeons in the country, he has worked selflessly. Mohamed Kallon's contribution to football is nationally acclaimed. The young inventor, Kelvin Doe, invited to do research at The Massachusetts Institute of Technology (MIT), was beaming with smiles at being honoured. Miriam Mason-Sesay came to this country in 1997 from Britain and after three years decided to stay. She started the Educaid chain of schools which now comprises one primary school and 4 secondary schools with 1700 pupils.

The ceremony was a mixture of exhilaration and sadness. Sahr Nbobor Saffa's 36-year service as a messenger had finally been noticed. Spare a thought also for serviceman John Kelli's widow as he was honoured post humously. She wept uncontrollably.

Oh, I almost forgot! I left out one notable awardee. I know I may be accused of being biased.This lady is not for turning. She set her sights some eighteen years back on running her own educational institutions. In 1995, she founded Modern Elementary school in Freetown after being thrown out of Sierra Rutile as a result of the rebel war. Within ten years she had also started a private secondary school, the Modern High School. Both schools are today amongst the foremost educational institutions in Sierra Leone. She employs over 80 staff and cares for over 1000 students. She also has considerable experience working with women empowerment groups, especially those dealing with the education of the girl child. She was also the proud recipient of the 2012 National Integrity Award from the Anti-Corruption Commission of Sierra Leone for her integrity in managing her own business in the educational sphere.

She has taught me that her students are the most important people in the education system  and puts paid to all limiting factors including poor performing teachers to ensure the students get a decent education. And lest I forget, I was her first bursar and resigned honourably when I got a job abroad. My friends used to advise her that the best way to audit the bursar was to search his back pocket after work!. In case you have not guessed, Mrs Helen Keili received an award for Officer of the order of the Rokel. I am very proud of my wife, They say behind every successful wife there is an id--t.

Ponder my thoughts

# May 7, 2013

## FINANCE MINISTRY, AGENCIES AND THEIR MONEY PALAVER

Balancing the budget is not an easy task for the finance ministry as it scrounges around to squeeze something out of every conceivable revenue source. That the ministry recently demanded that agencies, especially regulatory agencies, pay all licence and other fees directly into the Consolidated Fund is therefore not surprising. Some agencies like the National Telecommunications Commission (NATCOM) and the Sierra Leone Environmental Protection Agency (EPA-SL) do generate considerable revenue.

National regulatory agencies include NATCOM, EPA-SL, Sierra Leone Maritime Protection Agency (SLMA), Standards Bureau, National Minerals Agency (NMA) and many others. Some are in areas in which they may not be able to generate adequate funding easily. Others regulate sectors in which there are large and fairly well-heeled players. The finance ministry seems to be particularly concerned about the bigger, well-to-do regulators who in their opinion generate considerable funds.

There is concern however from the regulators that this will limit their operations significantly and not allow them to carry out their basic functions of monitoring and enforcement efficiently. Regulatory agencies deal in the area of administrative law, codifying and enforcing rules and regulations and imposing supervision or oversight for the benefit of the public at large. They are commonly set up to enforce standards and safety, or to oversee use of public goods and regulate commerce.

For quality regulation, such agencies need to have adequate human and technical resources. Agencies like EPA-SL, NMA and NATCOM are charged with overseeing highly sophisticated, technologically driven industries. To do so effectively, they would have to compete for personnel and resources in the same market as the companies they regulate. They may require more flexibility in terms of both methods and amounts of payment for specialized products and services. The rules that apply to the public sector civil service in general are often too restrictive for such agencies. I am well aware of how budgetary restrictions led to the poor performance of the environmental department, which was part of the lands ministry before EPA-SL was set up as an independent agency, even though licence fees were being collected. A study in which I was involved some years back concluded that even though the mines ministry collected some $7m in 2004 in terms of licence fees and other levies, the ministry was short of funds for monitoring and could not even buy consumables for the Geological survey lab as everything went directly into the consolidated which, with other competing social demands could be a big black hole.

It is clearly for reasons of independence and efficiency that such agencies are set up. A recent study on removing the administrative barriers to doing business in Sierra Leone gave the following opinion on regulators in Sierra Leone:

*"A trend is visible to give licensing fees a bigger role in the budgetary considerations and increase them across the board........The primary purpose of a license should be to guarantee compliance with certain regulations that aim to protect the health, safety and/ or the environment. The Main focus of a license should be consumer protection...................It should not be used for revenue purposes and the fee must go directly to the agency administering the license."*

The system of making regulators keep funds collected could have its challenges. Regulators themselves could make fees inordinately high and be unduly concerned with revenue generation. Also, the regulator may be susceptible to government interference and special government demands for "donations" or funding of pet projects. With proper governance of these agencies, these can be resisted. In cases where surpluses arise, the agency may retain the funds for its use, in which case licence fees could be reduced in future. Regulators should be well governed and kept in check. Despite their independence in substantive matters, regulatory agencies are like any other governmental bodies in regard to their obligations to be good stewards of public resources entrusted to them, to be accountable for their actions, and to operate on a reasonably efficient basis. They should be subject to a budget approval process and audit oversight. The performance of regulators must also be reviewed periodically.

The finance ministry should carefully consider its stance on this issue and grant some financial flexibility to agencies to build up their capacity and monitor and enforce the rules in their areas of operation. The NMA compromising on checking on mine dams, that could potentially kill a considerable number of people if they fail, or the EPA allowing some deleterious substance to contaminate public water supply for a community are inexcusable. Clearly our regulatory agencies must be well funded and run efficiently. Government should not relent on providing oversight but should not use these agencies as cash cows.

## LIES, DAMN LIES, STATISTICS AND POLITICS

The wife of a man who had five children and wanted no additional child got pregnant, much to her husband's chagrin. Unfortunately he read a report that said "every sixth child born in Africa is a Nigerian". Perplexed, he ran straight home to his wife. "You are going to have an abortion!" he exclaimed. "I am not going to have a Nigerian in this house!" Oh, the folly of statistics!

I listened to an interesting interview on Radio Democracy in which Mahmoud Idriss of ITASCAP, an integrated financial services company in Sierra Leone, and Monica Timbo of Campaign for Good Governance (CGG) struggled to explain statistical information related to a survey they had undertaken to assess the perception of people on their living conditions. A random sample of 1900 adults had been interviewed and their responses seemed to indicate that their lives were better off than twelve months ago.47 percent described the economic condition as "much better or better" and 46 percent as "very bad or fairly bad". 51 percent considered their living conditions "much better or better" and only 40 percent considered their living condition to be worse off: "very bad or fairly bad".

The government was also given pass marks in fighting corruption (54 percent), addressing educational concerns (52 percent), managing the economy (52 percent), providing water and sanitation services (51 percent and reducing crime (51 percent). There were other fairly damning statistics given but listeners were too preoccupied with these statistics, which seemed to indicate things were getting better. How could they interview only 1900 people to give their views for 6 million people? Did they interview more people from the North who were likely to be APC or the South who were likely to be SLPP? Had not CGG tarnished its reputation by subscribing to such a report? Mahmoud and Monica answered the questions well, using statistical lingo like sample sizes, confidence intervals, rejection of anomalous results etc. Mahmoud did mention that perception is what was measured and that there was no attempt to tie the results in with current socio economic statistics. At the end I could sense you had a very sceptical public.

"Scientific" data are often used in political debates to show how one political position is "better" than another. Statistics however confuses people. The Independent Radio Network (IRN) results at election time merely provide transient figures at various polling stations with no accompanying explanation or summary. People find the concept of moving averages confusing. "We were sitting at 55 percent. How come we are now at 45 percent?" they complain. Sometimes we are not sure whose statistics to believe. The Public Sector Reform Unit, the Ministry of

Education and the teachers' union could not agree on the number of ghost teachers- a maximum figure of 7000 has been proffered. But then ghosts are phantom beings!

The government sometimes uses statistics to its advantage but may often be too quick on the draw. The GDP growth rate for 2012 was initially projected at fifty-something percent then dropped to thirty-something percent and finally to a much lower figure. In the case of electricity, figures are put out with no attempt to classify the type of power. Usually figures are put out for installed capacity because they give the highest figures. Little attempt is made to explain to people that power from Bumbuna for example varies according to the season or that for power supply you will need to have standby units. Firm power (which can be guaranteed) could therefore be considerably lower.

I had a friend in Tongo who would always call for a "quarter dozen bottles of STAR" to impress people. Others belabour the point unnecessarily "52 percent of the population are female, therefore 48 percent are male" Of course there are no hermaphrodites!

Using statistics to distort is a worldwide phenomenon. Christopher Pollitt of Erasmus University, on a visit to Finland, was surprised to discover a category of prison - open prisons - with no escapes, ever. "You never have anyone escape from an open prison?" he asked an official. "Oh no, but because they are open prisons we don't call it an escape, we classify them as absent without leave."

Back to the report! Even I could not understand how 51 percent of the population could be enthused about their living conditions when we have a poverty rate close to 70 percent. But then there could be lot of satisfied poor people!-"Blessed are the poor..." I am also not certain how germane some questions may be for a rural person. Like assessing government's fight against corruption or reducing crime. The report did suggest however that the next urgent steps for government were to narrow income gaps, create jobs and keep prices down. To me this is what is important. Let's forget all that statistics and take an object lesson from the little boy who was asked the question "If you have ten sheep on one side of the road and five cross over when they see an approaching car, how many are left behind?". "None" he answered. He disputed his teacher's answer of five by observing, "You may know mathematics, Sir, but I know sheep better".

Ponder my thoughts

# May 28, 2013

## MOMODU MALIGI, WATER, PRIVATE SECTOR AND PREGNANCY.

It was good to see the Ministry of Water Resources have a business dialogue on the theme "Water is Everybody's Business" with the private sector recently. The sector could play a more significant role. It is engaged in construction of water supply facilities, repair of pumps, consultancy services, selling of drinking water and of products like pipes, tanks etc.

The need for investment in the water sector is huge. An annual investment of US$164 million is needed for new urban and rural water supply facilities, and rehabilitation of existing facilities. Compared with anticipated public financing, the projected minimum deficit totals over US$130 million per year for the water supply subsectors. Mechanisms for sustaining services are inadequate, in particular for the maintenance of existing water supply facilities.

Despite recent progress, just 57.1 percent of households in Sierra Leone have access to and use improved drinking water sources and 13.8 percent of households have water on their premises. 20.4 percent require 30 minutes or more to obtain drinking water, which burden women and girls as primary water collectors. Disparities in water coverage are clearly observed between rural and urban-the situation is considerably worse in rural areas.

The new Minister of Water Resources, Momodu Maligi, though quite upbeat about the future underscored the extent of the work to be done in a recent statement:

"I have no doubt that those targets that we have now set ourselves in the Agenda for Prosperity will surely be achieved. These challenge us to ensure that 74% and 66% of our population have access to improved water supply and improved sanitation respectively by 2017. That, unfortunately will still leave an estimated 1.8 million and 2.3 million of our people without access to any improved water supply and adequate sanitation respectively, and we owe them a duty to address their needs ahead of 2025, the year Africa's Shared Water Vision enjoins us to have universal coverage."

The government's plans for the sector have been fairly well laid out for urban and rural water supplies. For urban water supply it would undertake the preparation of an extensive investment plan with a mix of funds, to speed up reform of the sector to improve efficiency of cost recovery and set realistic tariffs to recover a substantial portion of production cost. Community ownership and management will be encouraged for rural water supply and the capacity of the private sector built up to provide goods and services. Major reforms include shifting government focus from implementer to policy making and facilitation, creation of a National Water Resources Board with responsibility for water resources management, establishment of a regime for regulating water supply and the enactment of a new Water Law which creates a legislative framework for all those involved in the sector. For these plans to work the ministry would need to avoid a fragmented approach to water resources management.

Urban water supply services face considerable challenges. The Guma Valley Water Company has been undergoing reforms but services to Freetown are still grossly inadequate. Try as they might, they need assistance in areas such as maintenance, metering, billing and pipe connection/disconnection. An area which was of particular interest mentioned by the minister was the possibility of utilising groups of trained youths in urban areas to manage water leakage and illegal connections and other functions in various communities in urban areas. They would be assigned specific areas and would not only guard against vandalism but would be responsible for repairing pipes to stop excessive leakages.

There are also opportunities for the private sector in rural water supplies. There are several reasons for the poor coverage and slow progress in rural areas, including: insufficient rates of capital investment, poor sustainability (non-functioning systems) due to lack of ongoing investment from users, limited local maintenance and management capacity; and limited (or no) ongoing external support. A local mechanic can be trained to operate pump maintenance. UNICEF has commenced the rolling out of a hand pump spares parts supply chain in eight districts targeting more than 4,107 partially damaged water points. The hand pump spares supply chain aims at strengthening the private sector and capacitating communities through village and savings loan schemes to make the operation and maintenance of water sources, affordable and sustainable.

All of these plans may be good but would obviously need the institutional framework and responsibilities to be clearly defined. Financing of such schemes should also be well thought through and people should be made to pay for water services. The Local Government Act (2004) devolved water supply functions to local councils. Under this system, central government grants are allocated to councils to cover activities such as construction, rehabilitation, and drilling of boreholes, spring wells, and other systems. Funds allocated however are grossly inadequate. Also there seems to be a grey area between the functions of Sierra Leone Water Company (SALWACO) and the local councils.

It is quite obvious that private industry can be made to play a significant role in the water sector so that water provision is improved in both urban and rural areas. Policy makers and implementers may have to think out of the box to achieve these objectives. The new minister has a lot on his hands and we hope his initial enthusiasm will be translated into concrete actions. He certainly needs the support of his colleagues at allied ministries such as local government and health and sanitation and also the political support from the top. It would help considerably if procurement guidelines are not contravened. Also, government should speed up the setting up of the new Electricity and Water Regulatory Commission.

Water and Private sector? But what about the pregnancy bit? Honourable Gladys Gbappi Brima of Moyamba District brought this issue to the fore recently. In households without a drinking water source on the premises, it is women and girls who collect water. In the 12 percent of households where children collect water, girls are twice as likely as boys to be responsible for collecting water. Young girls walk significant distances at odd hours to fetch water for their families, exposing them to the risk of physical assaults, rape and sexual violence. Water is a basic need and quality of access has important externalities on health, gender equality and environment justifying high political interest.

## INDEPENDENT POLICE COMPLAINTS BOARD? - GO POLICE!

"Go police!" has been etched into our national lingo. The genesis is quite well known. It is not however funny to the Police as many would say that despite their best efforts, they are still disparaged. Poor police!

Little wonder then that in his speech as chairman of the occasion for launching the nationwide pre-legislative sensitisation campaign on the setting up of the Independent Police Complaint Board (IPCB), the deputy minister of internal affairs, Sheka Tarawallie, was at pains to convince the police that despite what would seem to be public misgivings about them, they were dearly appreciated by the government. Here are a few quotes from the Minister's speech:

"I would like to state that this draft bill should not be seen as an indictment on the police; but as an inducement for more professional work. This is why, hand in hand with this proposed

bill, we are also putting the final touches to another document that primarily looks at the improvement of the welfare, terms and conditions of serving personnel in the Sierra Leone Police"
"Special congratulations to the Inspector General of Police and all members of the Sierra Leone Police. And just the other day, I heard Parliament heaping praises on the police force for financial transparency and accountability. More congrats!"

Enough of the platitudes and back to business! According to the minister, "The current status quo in Sierra Leone of the police investigating the police through the CDIID [Complaint Discipline and Internal Investigations Department] is certainly not enough. The public will never be satisfied if their complaints against police officers are also or just handled by police officers..........The answer lies in the setting up of an independent police complaints board, manned wholly and solely by civilians, with a running secretariat purposely devoted to investigating complaints from members of the public with regards police excesses. "
Lack of police accountability is fundamentally damaging to society. The public loses trust in the police and people resort to alternative means of protection and justice. Complaints against the police have been well publicised and the past few years have seen a considerable number of mishaps, including shootings which have left people dead or wounded.

The formation of the Independent Police Complaint Board would certainly seem to be justified. There is however a primary concern from the statement of the minister that the board may only deal with serious cases. The Minister stated thus: "It has to be said that the IPCB does not end the work of the CDIID, as the former would only deal with very serious complaints like deaths and injuries resulting to contacts with the police, or matters that the commission would deem necessary to investigate." What about other cases of gross injustice or police misconduct that may need independent scrutiny?

Whatever the eventual format it may take a lot of concerns may need to be addressed: Would the board have the investigative ability to effectively deal with police complaints? What happens if poor co-operation from the police hinders investigations? Will the board have the powers to ensure that the police comply with their recommendations? Will the Board be given sufficient resources to fulfil their mandate?

IPCB or not, it is imperative that the police are professional and politically neutral (that is, free from political manipulation), human rights orientated, democratic. obey the laws of the country, community-oriented and accountable. This is the real challenge facing them at the moment. These need to be addressed if we are not to be told: Go Police!

Ponder my thoughts

# June 3, 2013

## PUBLIC ACCOUNTS COMMITTEE: BOXING WITHOUT GLOVES

*"We hang the petty thieves and appoint the great ones to public office"*-
Aesop

I have been enthralled by the recent investigations of the Parliamentary Public Accounts Committee (PAC) into the misuse of state funds. Deputy Speaker of Parliament and Committee Chairman Chernor Maju Bah, his deputy, Komba Koedoeyema, and their committee should be congratulated for bringing the issue of accountability to the fore. The hearings have revealed perplexing information on the pervasive lack of accountability in the use of government funds. We have learnt that the Immigration Department banked considerably less money than it raised. In the then Ministry of Energy and Water Resources, there was inadequate control over distribution of fuel, amounting to Le 29,997,500, which was issued to a vehicle named 'Contingency Truck' whose existence the audit team could not verify. Bo school and some 13 schools in Bo could not account for a considerable amount of school fees and other moneys collected. In the case of the Bo City Council the investigations resulted in the incarceration of the chief administrator who was sentenced by the Committee to spend three days in detention for "lying under oath".

The recent Auditor General's report estimated that there had been cash losses to the public purse of Le 110,914,263,391 (approximately $26 million). The Audit Service Sierra Leone (ASSL) is mandated by the Constitution to audit and report on the public accounts of Sierra Leone and of all public offices including the courts, the accounts of central and local government administrations, universities and public institutions of like nature, any statutory corporation, company or the body or organization established by an Act of Parliament or statutory instrument or otherwise set up partly or wholly out of Public Funds. In this vein, the ASSL had to audit 39 ministries and departments, 19 local councils, 149 chiefdom authorities, 64 statutory bodies and donor funded projects. This is huge work and they should also be applauded for their comprehensive report on which the PAC is acting.

The issues cited in the Auditor General's report were way too numerous, the funds so huge and the trail so labyrinthine that considerably more work needs to be done by various bodies. The Anti Corruption Commission and civil society should also be in the avant garde of this fight. Truth be told, the PAC's capacity for investigation is limited. The committee has very little support staff with the requisite experience to assist them. Another major flaw especially on issues dealing with local government units is that these could be better handled by District Budget Oversight Committees (DBOCs). These DBOCs have however been largely impotent and are poorly staffed with members who have not appropriate skills to carry out these functions. One can also argue that if initiatives like the Public Expenditure Tracking Survey (PETS) were really effective they could help to close the stable door.

The auditor general, Lara Taylor-Pearce, has been unequivocal in stating that there has to be a more systematic approach to addressing this problem. A few self-explanatory excerpts from her report make this issue very clear:

"I am intent and hope that the government and all public officials will address the profound need to implement the very basics of internal control and to address the public financial management issues that my predecessor and I have been reporting for many years and on which progress has been snail-paced at best."

Some of the matters cited by her as being common to all ministries, departments and agencies (MDAs), Councils and Schools include:

- Payments without any or inadequate supporting documents.
- Monthly bank reconciliations not prepared.
- Fixed Asset registers not maintained or up to date.
- No or ineffective Internal Audit units.
- Failure to comply with procurement law and regulations is endemic.

She suggests a simple and effective way of reconciling cask book records to bank statements on a regular basis-"There is very little skill involved in preparing bank reconciliation. With procedures and forms it can be taught in less than a day to any clerk with basic numeracy and does not need the training of a professional accountant...... The return on a very small training investment to do bank reconciliations for a large number of selected public officials across the country would be enormous and should be undertaken without further delay."

One may want to ask the PAC if there is anything being done to follow up on these recommendations. Also what is being done about the following major players whose weaknesses have also been cited in the Auditor General's report?

"Governance at the National Revenue Agency is weak and systems of internal control there are still weaker. Indeed the internal financial control and administrative weakness of the NRA places compliance with the government's tax law and policy at risk of being disregarded if not ignored by the citizens and corporate taxpayers of Sierra Leone."

".........we continue to believe that administrative and financial management of the school system is out of control.

Responsibility and accountability rests squarely on the Ministry of Education and it is from there that corrective action needs to be initiated as a matter of the gravest urgency."

If these multifarious issues are not addressed, the PAC would be merely scratching the surface. It is time to device and implement a more holistic way of addressing issues raised in the Auditor General's report if such negative reports are not to continue for many more years.

## THE GREEN BOTTLE CONCLAVE WITHOUT A POPE

White smoke is seen emanating from the Sistine Chapel chimney, the bells begin pealing minutes after, signifying the election of a new pope. Later out comes a cardinal to pronounce "habemus papam" -"We have a Pope". This confirms the election of a new pope after the secret conclave of cardinals. Thankfully, the Noble Sarjorski Conclave has a simpler method of electing its head. There is nothing much secretive about a conclave that started over beer, roast beef, goat meat and pepper soup. We learn from recent newspaper reports that the conclave met in Makeni recently outside its normal domain of Liverpool Street.

This is not the only such conclave in town. Other famous watering holes have had their informal conclaves. These beer meetings are in nondescript bars with spartan facilities. It is no secret that there is one at Pademba Road and we have a famous one at Guy Street, which I myself frequent. The Guy street one has got so organised over the years that we have our usual Christmas carnival and Easter beach party. Such conclaves bring people together in an informal atmosphere. They usually provide the opportunity for well-heeled people from judges, politicians, ministers and professionals to hobnob in an informal atmosphere. It is also surprising how much political tolerance is displayed. It seems like the beer lubricates other parts of the body other liquids cannot reach and deadens their sense of bigotry of whatever sort.

Now back to the Noble Sarjoski conclave. An article by Titus Boye Thompson ("Conclave accepts Transforming Challenge" published in Awareness Times, May 31, 2013) tells us "the conclave had its roots from the kiosk once owned and operated by the late Sarjoh Bah at Wallace Johnson Street opposite the nurses hostel...." It is a social and networking organisation that now meets regularly at the premises of Mrs Jalloh on Liverpool Street.

It was a big honour for the whole group to be invited to what the grapevine says was an all expenses paid bash in Makeni. Time may yet tell whether the famous Pademba Road conclave and the Guy street one will follow this example. But who knows? They may produce a President one day!

The sceptic may ask why would prosperous people abandon all the posh places to sit in a less than pristine place drinking beer and munching various creatures "great and small". The answer, in my view lies in the need for camaraderie. Some overseas members of the Guy Street conclave have been known to pass through for their "pinta" before getting home after landing at Lungi airport. There is no set agenda but you do have great conversation. Because of the type of people frequenting the conclave you can almost rest assured that the dictum on the famous bar sign "When you come here, what you see here, what you say here, let it stay here" will be respected.

Sarjoski has gone places however. According to Boye Thompson, President Koroma? spoke about "a duty and a responsibility for its members to have regards to those less fortunate in society "How laudable! He also urged members to "raise their game and make the conclave relevant in society as a forum for influencing policy and instrumental in the development of new ideas for business and entre-preneurship."

As long as serious affairs of state are not sanctioned here over a pint of beer, who cares! The new chairman, Christopher John, talked about rebranding the conclave and getting involved in humanitarian and charitable works. He said the conclave had plans for securing landed property to have its own building.

A critic has said that the membership is now bloated (both in numbers and in the size of their stomachs) and there are more people joining now for political reasons. Based on his observation that it is an APC affair, which one of my APC friends vehemently denies, I am going to place my applications soon and will keep you posted on its progress or lack thereof.

Sahjoski conclave has come a long way and I am pleased that after so many years they can say "habemus praesidentem"-"we have a President". Should there be any white smoke from the chimney however, it can only be from the roasting of a goat!

Ponder my thoughts

# June 11, 2013

## DECENTRALISATION QUANDARY: MUSA TARAWALLI VS J.S.KEIFALA

The recent demolition of structures along the main streets of Kenema brings to the fore the problems between central government ministries and local councils. The mayor of Kenema City Council, J.S. Keifala, summed it all well when he challenged the demolition exercise engendered by the Minister of Lands, Country Planning and the Environment, Musa Tarawalli (Standard Times May 23, 2013- Kenema District Council challenges illegal land demolition): "We are embarrassed...Councils are the highest political entities in the regions and as such there is every need for any Ministry intending to carry out any action whether legal or illegal to inform and involve the councils."

This is symptomatic of the quagmire created by a half-hearted decentralisation process in which ministries want to preserve their turf, oblivious of the responsibilities of local councils and the spirit of the decentralisation process. This thread runs through other functions ostensibly devolved to local councils. It also does not help when you have local councils of one political stripe and a central government of another stripe in a heightened and poisoned political atmosphere.

The aim of decentralization was partly to improve public service delivery and partly to empower local communities to handle their own affairs. Yet, out of 80 functions slated for devolution, fourteen still remain to be devolved. Even some of those which have been devolved are in name only and to all intents and purposes controlled by central government. Areas for devolution include key services such as primary education, basic health care, agricultural services and maintenance of feeder roads.

Local councils however have very limited scope for revenue generation and rely largely on transfers from the central government. Such transfers are based on an allocation formula which restricts the spending autonomy of local councils, as grants are mainly earmarked. With the exception of a small number of core administrative staff, most of the service delivery staff are still on central government payroll, but report to local councils.

Whereas political decentralization is advanced and administrative decentralization may be improving, fiscal decentralization lags behind. Funds allocated to local government units are a very small percentage of the total national budget. Critics of our governance system also argue that until you make the local councils almost financially independent, they will be at the beck and call of central government. They add that the system of getting grants from central government will always be subject to partisan manipulation. The moribund Local Government Service Commission (LGSC) with responsibilities for managing the human resources of local councils would also need to be overhauled.

Some major functions of ministries which were supposed to be handed over to the local councils are still being run by the ministries. For the lands ministry these include land surveying, land registration and control of illegal sale of land, leasing of government land and preparation of land use plans. It is not abundantly clear under whose purview street stalls fall in local governance areas. Should it be under lands or the local council or should it even be a law and order issue under the purview of the police? In terms of consultation with market stall owners to get their buy-in, should not trade and industry be involved? It is clear that there may be many differences of opinion on how such issues should be handled in a governance system that is evolving and in which responsibilities may overlap.

Whatever the case, the lack of consultation between the lands ministry and the local council did not help the situation and may reek of disrespect. If reports are to be believed, the demolition exercise itself may have been executed lawlessly. According to one report, "Youths hired by the Ministry held big hammers, wheel pullers, roof cutters, demolishing stalls, kiosks and other makeshift structures under the watchful eyes of OSD [Operation Support Division] Police Officers." The whole issue begs several questions. Was the absence of consultation and the seeming brazen disregard for following normal procedures because the council was an SLPP governed council? Could more stakeholders have been consulted and the affected parties given enough notice to vacate these areas? This may be an isolated incident but what if this practice becomes the norm?

On the flip side, it could also happen that a local council refuses a legitimate request from a ministry or fails to cooperate on an issue that is legitimately within the purview of a ministry to undermine a government of a different political stripe. All of these are genuine issues with which we should grapple if our governance system is to thrive. One keen observer has opined that perhaps we should be moving towards having a local governance system not based on parties. This is not far-fetched and is certainly an issue that should be brought to the table.
As he noted, "the Ministry would not have broken stalls in Makeni without consulting with the Council."

## TEENAGE PREGNANCY: PREGNANT WITH EXPECTATION

There has always been a quiet rivalry between my mother's village (Mobai) and my father's (Baiima), three miles apart in the Kailahun District. In the days of the train and rural post offices (yes, there used to be post offices!), letters addressed to Mobai were labelled "Mobai via Baiima". Then the railway disappeared and in came the Vianini road which went as far as Pendembu, bypassing Baiima but going through Mobai. Letters to Baiima were now addressed "Baiima via Mobai" because Mobai now had the post office. So much for Kailahun development history! The rivalry has continued over the years and I and my siblings have tried hard not to take sides. A few years back there was an invitation from a benefactor for a girl in the primary school at Baiima to go to the United Kingdom on a short bursary. This was good news that was gleefully communicated to folks at Mobai. The day of travel was fast approaching but we had one small problem-the girl who was to be the recipient got pregnant. There were hurried attempts to draft in a substitute but the others were also pregnant. They finally settled on a student from the Mobai School. A case of "to the rival goes the spoils".

Teenage pregnancy is however no joking matter and is a scourge. I was pleased that President Koroma recently launched a campaign against the alarming rate of teenage pregnancy by the unveiling of a 'National Strategy for the Reduction of Teenage Pregnancy' (Standard Times- Thursday May 30-Sierra Leone making in-roads in the fight against teenage pregnancy.). Launched with the slogan; "Let Girls Be Girls and Not Mothers", the president said teenage pregnancy denies girls the benefits of education, and compromises a country's ability to secure gender equity, enhance growth and transform itself.

"Girls must be "book carriers, not baby carriers"", he added. The special guest of honour for the occasion was the first lady of Nigeria, Dame Dr. Patience Good luck Jonathan.

Snippets from the various speeches delivered are particularly relevant. Dame Patience Jonathan referred to the complications in pregnancy and child-birth as a major cause of death among teenagers. She said that during pregnancy and delivery, girls of 14 years old and much younger, face problems of anemia, acute malaria, pregnancy induced hypertension, obstructed labor, among others. The Executive Representative of the Secretary General of the United Nations (ERSG) to Sierra Leone, Jens Tourberg-Frandzen mentioned that in Sierra Leone every third child born has a mother who is herself a child and 40 percent of maternal deaths are teenagers.

Regionally, more than 50 per cent of adolescent girls give birth by age 20 (WHO 2010) In Sierra Leone, statistics of pregnant women aged 15-49 years, who were married or in consensual union indicates that 16 per cent were married before age 15, and 50 per cent before age 18. In addition, 24.5 per cent of women aged 15 to 19 years, started having sexual intercourse before age 15. The statistics in Mattru Jong is particularly disturbing. A total of 434 teenage pregnancies were recorded at the UBC hospital in Mattru Jong in the first half of 2011 of which 73 percent were school going girls.

There is a strong relationship between poverty and teenage pregnancy with teenage girls in the poorest quintile being three times more likely to have a child before age 18 years compared to girls in the wealthiest quintile. A UNICEF document (2010) identifies peer-pressure as a key determinant for adolescents, particularly young girls to indulge in unsafe behaviour, substance abuse and unprotected sex. Local experts speculate pregnancies are caused by voluntary sexual relations among school-children, early marriage, transactional sex with adults and other forms of sexual abuse.

Challenges to be addressed include gender-based violence, barriers to women's economic empowerment, inadequate sensitisation and education on gender and development issues. The establishment of a Sexual Offences court has also been mentioned.

Programmes should be devised to reduce the incidences of teenage pregnancy or help to reintegrate teenage mothers into productive life by continuing their education, skills training or accessing opportunities for employment or income generation. The setting up of the National Secretariat for the Reduction of Teenage Pregnancy within the Ministry of Health and Sanitation

(MOHS) under the coordination of a multi sectorial committee comprising the MOHS and MSWGCA-with the collaboration of UN agencies is a step in the right direction.

Perhaps we can realise the dreams of Information Minister Alpha Kanu who waxed poetical at the launching when he said "A daughter is the happy memories of the past, the joyful moments of the present and the hope and promise of the future."

I am pregnant-pregnant with expectation that we will set about addressing this scourge in a holistic way.

Ponder my thoughts.

# June 25, 2013

## OGI'S CITIZENS' REPORT CARD: WHO'S FOOLING WHO?

I really cherished the idea of reviewing the Citizens' Report Card (CRC) which ostensibly would give me as well as other Sierra Leoneans an indication of what the populace thinks about the government's delivery of public services. This effort by the Open Government Initiative (OGI) seemed a laudable one and I was assured from the introductory paragraphs that scientific procedures had been followed. OGI had contracted out the survey. The CRC survey was administered in all the 149 Chiefdoms and the Western Area. A total of 8050 respondents completed the questionnaire. Fifty respondents completed the survey in every chiefdom.

The report gives assesses the perception of citizens of some of the projects implemented under the President's Agenda for Change by key public sector institutions such as Education, Health and Sanitation, Infrastructure, Agriculture and Energy and Water Supply primarily and other areas of governance.

There are some responses that one would not dispute, especially in areas dealing with some aspects of infrastructure and agriculture. The report indicated that 89.7 percent of respondents were aware of the government's development of road networks and that 66.6 percent noted that the Government's road network initiative has improved movement and trade in localities. The assessment of infrastructure since 2008 was rated by 14 percent of respondents as excellent and by 60% as good. The positive appreciation of some aspects of Agriculture also seemed in place.

That is the positive news. My general conclusion after the review however indicates that many aspects of the report insult our collective intelligence. It would appear there were so many "leading" questions deliberately meant to elicit a favourable impression of the Government's agenda. Questions were inappropriate in many instances and some answers certainly defy logic. I will just point out a few for you to ponder.

The respondents' rating of the Government's Free Health Care (FHC) initiative indicates that 81.1 percent either consider it as excellent or good. The questions related to how it can be improved were bland at best and really could not elicit information that could be useful for government to act upon. One may not want to dispute the answers given but wonders whether the question should not have been framed differently to indicate how well the scheme was being implemented.

A question framed as "How frequent is electricity in your communities" yielded incredulous answers. In Kailahun and Kono which have no grid electricity, between 55 percent and 73 percent of respondents seem to have electricity more than once a week! Bo, which has grid electricity at least in Bo City fares worse than Kailahun and Kono. If on the other hand the question referred to any other form of electricity, including personal generators, then the question was either wrongly framed or daft. Why would you want to ask a man who has a personal generator how often he gets electricity? There was no attempt to frame any questions specific to rural electrification.

Sixty four percent of respondents think the educational system in Sierra Leone has improved. This seems to be markedly at variance with what we hear over the radio, read in newspapers and experience personally. Whatever the strengths of this government, education is certainly not one of them. The optional answers given respondents to the question, "What could be done to improve accessibility to primary education of the programs" are listed as follows: a) create more public awareness through OGI b) more community involvement c) improve monitoring and evaluation mechanisms d) improve planning and implementation e) other (specify). These seem very generic, like something drafted by some abstract M&E person. No wonder the top-most suggestion aimed at improving accessibility to primary schooling is to improve monitoring and evaluation mechanism as suggested by 31.8 % of the respondents. I can think of one dozen or more other more appropriate options that could have been offered for the answer but then I guess the intention was not really to find out.

There are other equally dubious answers related to other sectors. In the area of ICT, the survey indicates that four in every ten respondents are aware that Government has established a multi-purpose resource centre in Bo, Kenema, Makeni and Freetown. Furthermore, three in every ten respondents have benefited from the use of Government resource centres (from all 149 chiefdoms and the Western area!). I find it difficult to believe this. ICT literacy must be very high indeed! The survey also indicates that 24.5% of respondents have made use of the services of the Ombudsman's office-one out of every four persons! The ombudsman must be the busiest man in Sierra Leone, and Siaka Steven Street must be full of people waiting to see him!

Also, 69.8% of respondents support the Government's renegotiation of all mining and large scale investment agreements? Who negotiated them before the renegotiation? Is this a leading question to tell people the Government is seeking their interest in renegotiating contracts?

I vehemently disagree with the OGI Director's conclusion in her foreword to the report that "The report gives an effective evaluation of government performance, it has identified major constraints in service delivery and most important of all able to identify key recommendations that would enhance economic growth and development in this country."

I am disappointed in this report. I believe as Sierra Leoneans of whatever political stripe we should know exactly what is happening and endeavour to collectively address the situation. Tinkering with a report to show the Government in a positive light is a disservice to the Government itself and certainly does not give the President the correct picture. This is one spin that has gone too far in my opinion. I would have been very reluctant to make this report public. OGI should go back to the drawing board.

## IN DEFENCE OF THE BO SCHOOL "KONDOR"

A scathing report in Awoko newspaper recently highlighted the unhygienic condition of food served at Bo school- "Sierra Leone: Unhygienic food served in Bo school kitchen". The reporter was very graphic in describing the situation-"The water system is no longer working; the drainages are blocked and some broken down; and this condition gives the whole kitchen area a putrid smell...instead of using actual kitchen utensils the cooks use steel buckets that are replete with stains and rust--during the normal service of "kondor" (food for all) food is served from these same stained and rusty steel buckets."

My initial reaction was "Oh, how have the mighty fallen". The "kondor" used to be the pride of many boarding departments and the sumptuous meal was many a time "doubled". Undoubtedly it has contributed to the bulging biceps and stomachs of many a Bo School boy. I cannot imagine anyone in my days referring to "kondor" as "unhygienic". In my days at CKC the food was good, the workers well looked after, especially the cooks. There was certainly no talk of unhygienic food. Yes, a few beads of sweat may have found their way into the soup or "abobor" from a sweating Thermogene (yes, that was our cook's name), but not on the scale described by this zealous reporter when he says, "In the course of this, the cooks perspire so much because of the apparent use of the "kinetic energy". Kinetic energy indeed! The reporter also refers to the poor conditions of service of the cooks.

Time was, when Bo school had much less than four hundred students. Today it is double that number. Today, the problems in our educational system are immense. Many schools have resorted to having a double shift system. I know Bo school has resisted but this is being done at great inconvenience. The lack of books, poor infrastructure facilities, poor conditions of service and the low socio-economic status of people generally have meant that the educational system is under threat. Government does apportion some money directly as grants to Government Boarding secondary schools. This amounts to Le 4.5 billion but would have to be shared with several other schools-Kenema Magburaka etc. This may not be enough and the low Boarding home fees may not be enough to meet any shortfall.

Notwithstanding, the question that would have to be asked is whether those handling these funds are using them well. There have already been reports about the possible misuse of funds by school administrators at Bo school and other schools. Several questions come to mind. Is the procurement system for food in boarding schools above board? Are the school officials sufficiently accountable?

To their credit, alumni associations of many of these famous schools have been doing well for their schools. Associations for Grammar School, Prince of Wales, St. Edwards, Albert Academy, CKC, Bo School, Annie Walsh (market palaver notwithstanding) and others have been given significant support to their schools. I understand from some peeved Old Bo School Boys Association (OBBA) in the United States that their branch of OBBA alone donated some 400 mattresses recently and had at one time donated money for the refurbishment of the kitchen. OBBA has in the past built and equipped a library and done so much for the school.

This is all the more reason why I join the call for OBBA to support the MPBK (Movement for the Preservation of Bo School Kondor). The famous (probably more aptly infamous) "kondor" has played its part in shaping their future and should not be allowed to atrophy. As one famous Bo School boy was reputed to have said after "doubling", "obesity is the mother of invention". Unless OBBA intervenes the "necessity" may never arise for making that statement!

Ponder my thoughts.

# July 2, 2013

## FAILED STATE INDEX: A TALE OF TWO COUNTRIES

A recent report on state failure makes interesting reading. The Failed States Index is an annual ranking of 178 nations based on their levels of stability and the pressures they face. It is prepared by the Fund for Peace (FFP), an independent, nonpartisan, non-profit research and educational organization that works to prevent violent conflict and ensure sustainable security. It does this by analysing millions of documents every year. Scores are apportioned for every country based on twelve key political, social and economic indicators that can reinforce each other, pushing countries or communities into greater instability if not addressed. The lower the score, the higher the ranking and the better the performance. There is good news and not so good news for Sierra Leone in the 2013 ranking.

First the good news. The report states that two countries that illustrate how slow and steady success in state building really is are Sierra Leone and Timor-Leste. In the first Failed States Index in 2005, Sierra Leone was ranked 6th. In 2013, Sierra Leone has climbed down to 33rd, having improved over ten points in eight years. Our ranking of 33 means we trounce Ivory Coast (12), Guinea (14), Nigeria (16), Kenya (17) (Liberia (23) all of which are in the "High Alert" Category, with Sierra Leone in the "Alert" category together with Rwanda (38). The rankings go from very high alert, high alert, alert, very high warning, warning, less stable, stable, very stable, and sustainable to very sustainable. Of the African countries, only South Africa (113) Botswana (121) and Ghana (110) are classed under "Warning"-their highest category.

The not so good news. Neighbouring Gambia thrashes us at a ranking of 62 and in the "very high warning" category. The indicators used are compared below. The first score refers to Sierra Leone and the second, Gambia (the lower the score out of ten, the better the performance).

| | | |
|---|---|---|
| Demographic Pressures | 9.0, | 7.7 |
| Refugees and IDPs | 8.1, | 6.4 |
| Uneven Economic Development | 8.5, | 6.8 |
| Group Grievance | 5.9, | 3.7 |
| Human Flight and Brain Drain | 8.0, | 7.1 |
| Poverty and Economic Decline | 8.6, | 7.8 |
| State Legitimacy | 7.3, | 7.6 |
| Public Services | 9.0, | 7.5 |
| Human Rights and Rule of Law | 6.1, | 8,0 |
| Security Apparatus | 5.4, | 5.5 |
| Factionalised elites | 7.9, | 6.8 |
| External intervention | 7.4, | 6.9 |
| Total | 91.2, 81.8 | |

I will attempt to comment on four of these indicators.

***DEMOGRAPHIC PRESSURES*** - "Pressures on the population such as disease and natural disasters make it difficult for the government to protect its citizens or demonstrate a lack of capacity or will."

This includes pressures and measures related to natural disasters, disease, environment, pollution, food scarcity, malnutrition, water scarcity, population growth, youth bulge and mortality.

Our environmental problems - rampant deforestation etc., low access to water and sanitation and youth problems do not help our situation.

***UNEVEN ECONOMIC DEVELOPMENT*** -"When there are ethnic, religious, or regional disparities, governments tend to be uneven in their commitment to the social contract."

This includes pressures and measures related to GINI coefficient, Income share of highest 10%, Income share of lowest 10%, Urban-Rural service distribution, access to improved services and slum population.

A recent report on poverty in Sierra Leone from 2003 to 2011 indicates that although, national inequality levels have decreased yet 20 percent of the population controls about 50 percent of the economy. Little attempt is made to address our slum problems.

*POVERTY AND ECONOMIC DECLINE*- "Poverty and economic decline strain the ability of the state to provide for its citizens if they cannot provide for themselves and can create friction between the "haves" and the "have nots"."

This includes pressures and measures related to economic deficit, government debt, unemployment, youth employment, purchasing power, GDP per capita, GDP growth and inflation.

Although we lag behind Gambia in this area, recent high GDP figures attributable largely to the mining sector give some degree of hope. The report earlier cited on poverty indicates that "nationally, poverty has decreased from 66.4 to 52.9 percent between 2003 and 2011 – a reduction of more than 10 percent". Unemployment is however still very high.

*PUBLIC SERVICES*-"The provision of health, education, and sanitation services, among others, are key roles of the state." This includes pressures and measures related to Policing, Criminality, Education Provision, Literacy, Water & Sanitation, Infrastructure, Quality Healthcare, Telephony, Internet Access, and Energy Reliability.

We again lag behind Gambia in this area. Despite improvements in infrastructure, it behooves us to ensure these developments are sustainable. The healthcare system is under threat. There are however high hopes with telephony and internet access with the fibre optic scheme.

*HUMAN RIGHTS AND THE RULE OF LAW* -"When human rights are violated - unevenly protected, the state is failing in its ultimate responsibility."

This includes pressures and measures related to Press Freedom, Civil Liberties, Political Freedoms, Human Trafficking, Political Prisoners, Incarceration, Religious Persecution, Torture and Executions.

This is one area where we roundly trounce Gambia. Unlike Gambia, we have had no executions for a very long time. Our human rights record and press freedom credentials are much more respectable. Our religious tolerance is second to none. One caveat though- We should put paid to the recent police excesses.

This report should spur us to improve on weak areas. We have done well since 2003 and should applaud ourselves as the FSI report suggests, albeit with a dose of reality, that unless we have the right resolve, we may slip back. As the report says "Ultimately what the FSI teaches us is to be realistic and -- to an extent – to be patient. Certainly, countries can decline both rapidly and gradually. Without significant capacity and a high-level of resiliency, however, the road to recovery will be a long and rocky one, filled with potholes and setbacks."

## TODAY'S STUDENT LEADERS: TOMORROW'S ROGUISH LEADERS

The recent violence in Student Union elections at Fourah Bay College (FBC) is symptomatic of the indiscipline pervasive in our society. To many young people who have given up on the older generation, it is indeed a disappointment that students at the oldest university in the country seem to mirror the worst of society at large with their indiscipline and intolerance of each other's views.

Despite several attempts by young folks to explain the philosophy of the Blackman camp or the White man camp at FBC to me, I have never been able to fathom how they go by these names and what they stand for. There are a whole host of issues affecting the welfare of students which should preoccupy student unions if their executives could be elected and function properly, but many colleges do not even get to the stage of holding elections.

The authorities of the University of Sierra Leone have now banned student union elections on all of the three campuses - Fourah Bay College (FBC), College of Medicine and Allied Health Sciences (COMAHS) and Institute of Public Administration and Management (IPAM) - indefinitely because of the unruly behaviour of students during their elections. At FBC one source says "this included the disruption of manifesto presentations, smearing of a bucket load of human excrement on the door of the warden of students, publication of a nude photo of one of the presidential candidates for the Student Union elections, the use of invectives on political rivals, throwing of missiles at rival supporters, etc." The source also says "Politically overactive or overzealous students at IPAM and COMAHS also made life unbearable for fellow students and lecturers." Critics say that ethnicity and politics sometimes rear their ugly heads in these elections.

One observer quips "This is not the first time FBC students have used human excrement as a weapon against their political enemies (perceived or imaginary) during student union elections. The weapon was first deployed in early 2000 and since then, many innocent students and lecturers have suffered as a result its use. It is said to be a very effective 'biological' weapon."

How sad. So sad that a 1970s alumnus yearned for the good old days thus:

"Clearly a reflection of the society from whence they came. Very sad indeed. Back in my days, FBC was the bastion of democracy and democratic practices. Free and fair elections were the order of the day – policy-laden cam-paigns, manifestos, political rallies and debates. ...with all the humour that came with that. Yes, winning strategies were based on an understanding of the demographics. But you could still call it fair. No patently obvious coercion was tolerated. After elections, you could count on a universal response to a call to MOBILIZE. Ah, for the good              old              days!"

Poignant observations indeed!

When we have students aligning themselves along camps which have no well defined and credible ideology, when students resort to violence against other students, when students would not be tolerant to hear the views of each other, when these future leaders allow themselves to be manipulated by politicians or take action on issues depending on ethnicity, when financial malpractices become the norm in running their affairs, the young students should have little reason to complain. I shudder to think what they will do when they take over the reins of power in this country in future. All may not be lost however. Will students who exemplify the voice of reason please stand up and be counted? Could various groups like the Anti-Corruption Commission (ACC), Attitudinal and Behavioural Change (ABC) Secretariat, National Commission for Democracy (NCD) intensify their efforts to engender a paradigm shift in their attitudes? Should not politicians make a conscious effort to keep out of their politics?

Ponder my thoughts.

# July 9, 2013

## 2014 CENSUS: SLPP SAYS-"SEND ANOTHER MOSES"

The book of Numbers refers to a prominent feature of the forty years the Israelites took to reach the Promised Land, the two censuses performed. "The LORD spoke to Moses in the tent of meeting in the Desert of Sinai after the Israelites came out of Egypt. He said: "Take a census of the whole Israelite community by their clans and families, listing every man by name, one by one (Numbers 1:1-2). Apart from their military objective, the censuses had another. "The LORD said to Moses, "The land is to be allotted to them as an inheritance based on the number of names. To a larger group give a larger inheritance, and to a smaller group a smaller one; each is to receive its inheritance according to the number of those listed." (Numbers 26:52-54).

Censuses are as old as the hills and even in the days of Moses, people could organise them well and use them for planning purposes. Fast forward to 21st century Sierra Leone. There have been recent concerns about the oversight and management of Statistics Sierra Leone (SSL), the agency charged with the responsibility of demographic data collection and analysis, as well as allegations of impropriety in newspapers. Another census is due in 2014 to obtain reliable and up-to-date data for the country, the last one having been held in 2004. The fact that data from such a census will guide policy formulation, planning, resource allocation and boundary delimitation for both Parliamentary and Local Council elections is well known. The opposition Sierra Leone People's Party (SLPP) in a press release is however concerned about several issues.

Firstly, the SLPP claims that the Steering (advisory) and technical committees which should comprise various stakeholders, including representatives from all political parties are almost dysfunctional. Some important stakeholders as well as political parties have not been invited to join the steering committee, which meets infrequently. The press release also raises concerns about the composition of the Technical Committee and its infrequent meeting habits.

Secondly, SSL has not had an oversight board for the past three years. This seems to be corroborated by a report in Standard Times which reports that "the last Board was dissolved in 2010 and the substantive Chairman had his services terminated in 2011. Instead of recommending a new Board, the Minister of State, Finance and Economic Development (11) has continued to enjoy performing the supervisory role which could have been performed by the Board".

The release further states that there is no chief technical adviser (CTA) who should serve as an independent arbiter to oversee the census process.

Several other accusations are levied bordering on concerns about the ongoing cartographic mapping and the non transparent and skewed recruitment process for additional staff which is based on political loyalties.

In its newspaper report, Standard Times goes to the extent of "leaking" news on the recommendations of a consultant who was hired to undertake a review of the Institution. It states, "In 2012 on the recommendations of the then Minster of Finance and Economic Development, Dr. Samura Kamara, DFID recruited a Consultant, named Dr. Pepper and assigned him to SSL to undertake a review of the institution. The DFID Consultant.....recommended that the entire institution be restructured....and that the Statistician General, and the entire Management with the exception of the Cartographic Director and staff be relieved of their duties".

Mr Mohamed King Koroma Statistician General, SSL has refuted these allegations in an interview with Mysierraleoneonline as stated in the following excerpts:

"The Technical Committee, Census Advisory Committee all of them have been set up .........The appointment of the Chief Technical Officer (CTO) and the Independent Cartographic Expert formed part of the process. The vacant adverts for these positions have been prepared but are yet to be advertised including other positions".

"The Technical Committee has been inaugurated and they have met three times. The Steering Committee that also comprises members drawn from all facets of society including political parties has met two times. In all these two meetings, all the political parties were invited including SLPP but they failed to attend ".

On the issue of the Board he replied: "It is the government that appoints the Board. The DfiD Consultant, Dr. Pepper set up standards and recommendations on how the Board should be appointed....... As an institution, we are looking forward to the government to appoint new board."

On the issue of politicisation of appointments he noted: "Statistics Sierra Leone employs Sierra Leoneans not politicians".

It is obvious from his response that the Institution has no Board and that recommendations by the independent consultant have been put on the shelf at the moment. It is also puzzling that he claims the SLPP failed to attend meetings of the steering committee to which they were invited. This sound hollow at best.

The government should certainly step in to clarify this obfuscation on such an important national issue and not leave things to the Statistician General to lamely defend his turf. These are serious allegations against the government and an institution having stewardship of such an important area of our governance and a process so essential for maintaining parity in our tenuous democratic system.

What is in Pepper's report? Does it throw any pepper into the eyes of Government or SSL? The last census in 2004 resulted in less parliamentary seats in districts like Bonthe and Pujehun. Bonthe was particularly riled as it saw its parliamentary seats drop from 5 to 3. That these occurred in supposedly SLPP strongholds under SLPP's political watch is a credit to the party. Indeed let the chips fall where they may, as long as the process is credible. Introducing any bias into the system will not bode well for our nascent democracy.

The government needs to come out with responses to these allegations to assuage the fears of many discerning people. The last thing we want is to have another cause for one party to feel it is being treated unfairly, with the concomitant insecurity it could create.

Surely, we can do the decent thing to count ourselves correctly. Why should we wait until another Moses arrives to address this serious situation and take us to the Promised Land?

## SL SANITATION: THE "NUMBER 2" PROBLEM IS SERIOUS

A recent article in the Washington Post titled "Unsanitary conditions seem to be frustrating attempts to help world's malnourished children" caught my attention. According to the writer, scientists increasingly suspect that constant exposure to bacteria, virus and parasite-laden faecal contaminants may be frustrating attempts to end malnutrition. The best diet-based measures to fight chronic hunger in the developing world are being negated by a failure to meet basic human needs; clean water and sanitation. He asserts: "A gut constantly assaulted by infections is less adept at absorbing nutrients for growth and development". My mind raced to the obvious implications related to our dire sanitation problems.

I am loathe to discuss issues of bowel disengagement in a public forum but it is so important we have to talk about it. I will try to be as civilised as middle class British when they refer with a stiff upper lip to a "wee" as "Number 1" and bowel emptying as "Number 2". I rather prefer these to another civilised description of a friend of mine as opening a "current account" or "deposit account" respectively in a "Bank". No prizes for guessing what a bank is!

Seriously speaking, the Number 2 problem is grave in Sierra Leone and has serious health implications. The correlation between health and water and sanitation is indisputable.

I will set the scene by distinguishing between the different types of "Banks" which are classed as "improved", "unimproved" and "non-improved" flush to piped sewer system; flush to septic tank; flush to pit latrine; flush to somewhere else; VIP (ventilated Improved Pit -not very important person!) latrine; composting toilet. "Unimproved": pit latrine with slab; open pit latrine (no slab); hanging toilet/latrine; other. "None": no facilities / bush / field; bucket.

In rural areas, close to 30% of people have sanitation facilities classed as "none" and less than 5% as "improved". In Freetown about 5% have "none" and only about 17% are in the improved category. In Freetown, especially, sanitation problems abound in well developed communities which are surrounded by shanty houses, many without toilet facilities. A friend of mine had an ingenious method of ending a "Bank" war. Some shady neighbours who incessantly put their "deposit accounts" into plastic bags and posted them over the fence into his compound were astounded when he started "returning them to sender". The war stopped!

Truth be told, there are many initiatives currently being undertaken, especially to address the "Number 2" problem. One such initiative was recently undertaken in nineteen communities in Moyamba District which were declared Open Defecation Free (ODF).

The Sanitation Project was started in 2012 by development aid organization, CORD-SL with support from UNICEF. A newspaper report says "Magbenka, Motonku-Loko and other communities were declared ODF". The superintendent of the Moyamba District Health Management Team mentioned that Magbenka village was the first community that recorded an outbreak of Cholera in 2012 which led to several deaths.

CORD embarked on a massive education campaign on sanitation in thirty communities in the Moyamba district and constructed several water wells. The District Health superintendent called on the people to stop using streams and backyards as toilets and urged the Council to continue to monitor communities to ensure that they are ODF.

Considering the scale of the problem, projects like this need to be replicated if we are to address the "Number 2" problem. We need to have sensitisation campaigns and more "Improved Banks". The sceptic may very well ask-Where are the sanitary inspectors of old? Why can we not make the "Number 2" problem a law and order issue with punitive measures? What are our long terms plans for central sewage systems in urban areas?

Ponder my thoughts.

# July 16, 2013

## ENGENDER THE AGENDA!

Over the past decade, Sierra Leone has implemented three generations of Poverty Reduction Strategy Papers. The IPRSP in 2001, the first generation from 2004-2007, and the second generation from 2008-2012 (Agenda for Change). The recent National Conference on Development and Transformation has led to the Agenda for Prosperity (AFP) which was launched by President Koroma last Friday.

According to the president, for the next five years, the new agenda will be the road map towards meeting our goal of becoming a middle income country and donor nation within the next 25 to 50 years. To dispel criticism that the previous Agenda for Change has many issues that still remain unaddressed he admitted in his speech, "We will do more to complete residual projects in the Agenda for Change and to address recurring and emerging challenges".

 The AFP will probably be a good document that outlines well thought out national plans that should ostensibly lead us to "the promised land". On paper the goals and analytical objectives may be desirable and well articulated and the plans may be acceptable. The sceptic may however be excused for having that nagging feeling that without addressing some fundamental issues, the AFP may become a pie in the sky.

The AFP depends a lot on the meaningful growth of the private sector. However, access to capital, legal impediments, bureaucracy, and poor infrastructure services will continue to thwart the private sector unless they are seriously addressed.

The extractives sector is slated to play a large part in funding the AFP. Proper and prudent management of the extractives sector is absolutely necessary. We cannot however depend ad infinitum on finite resources and there is need for a marked diversification of our economy beyond the minerals sector.  The President seemed to reflect this in his speech: "Abundance of natural resources is only half the story; the reality of prosperity only comes to a people that go for it....We must ensure that our economy is diversified to promote inclusive and sustainable growth. We must anchor our Agenda on efforts at being globally credible and internationally competitive."

It is important that greater emphasis is put on implementation and monitoring issues for all programmes proposed under the AFP. It is reassuring that this issue received mention in his speech: "Emphasis will be placed on monitoring of projects to ensure that results are achieved on timely manner. We will continue to attract foreign direct investment by forging strong partnerships with the private sector, especially on large-scale projects.

Its implementation will be guided by strong commitments by Development Partners as well as the Government."

Human capacity building is a common thread that affects the operation of various sectors of our economy. This again received mention: "This (the AFP) may require partnerships with internationals in building up capacities in our judiciary, our foreign ministry and other key state institutions. To be successful in the global environment we need to draw upon the best and committed within the country, the best and committed within the Diaspora and the best and committed at the global level."

Corruption is still a major problem. It was however disappointing that he skated over this issue in his speech.

Transforming Sierra Leone into a middle income country may be a laudable aim, but we must approach things with a dose of reality. There are still many issues that remain unaddressed in the Agenda for Change and even the coordinators of the Millennium Challenge Coordinating Unit (MCCU) acknowledge that realising the AFP vision may be a fairly tall order. In their presentation of a diagnostic study of the Sierra Leone economy to the President a week before the AFP launch they stated: "Sierra Leone has maintained a modest growth trajectory over the past (average 6%); however, the gradient of this trajectory needs to dramatically (average 13%) increase to achieve the targeted middle income status in the next 2 to 3 decades." The mining boom which fuels the current high growth rate is ephemeral and we would need accelerated growth in other sectors.

The conclusions of the MCCU report on our binding constraints certainly provide food for serious thought:

"1. The lack of adequate, reliable and affordable access to electricity supply to support the emergence and growth of a wide range of economic activities.

**2.** The extremely poor conditions of secondary and feeder road networks, which provide access to highly productive regions of the country with even higher potentials to drive growth.

3. The low quality and availability of Water and Sanitation coupled with the high incidence of waterborne diseases lead to high health expenditures and days lost due to such diseases, hence impacting negatively on worker productivity.

4. The access and cost of Land is high and that the policy and institutional issues surrounding private investments are poor."

Welcome, Agenda for Prosperity! A word of caution though-There may be light at the end of the tunnel, but who knows if it is a train approaching?

## THE TI REPORT: MUCH ADO ABOUT SOMETHING

In a recent report by Transparency International (TI) on bribery in several countries, Sierra Leone suffered the ignominy of coming first. Sierra Leone had the highest incidence of bribery, more particularly with respect to accessing social services (the Police, justice, health, education, licenses, registration and electricity). The airwaves were inundated with Government functionaries leaping to our defence.

The basic defence depended on the premise that you cannot have 1000 persons give views for a population of six million. The Minister of Information and Communications appeared to be the lead Defence Council. "They must have gone to Country lodge to interview people. They did not even consider the views of people like Mammy Yeabu at Kurobola."

A senior APC supporter claimed on an internet discussion forum: "The bribe money was for the private pockets of the individual bribed officials and not for the benefit of the government."-obviously this person only regards government as being composed of Cabinet Ministers. An article in Cokorioko was the icing on the cake: "How many times must it be drummed home to these organisations that in these guided polls people often lie, exaggerate or even deliberately misinform depending on their state of mind at the time" the writer asserts.
For the benefit of naysayers let us take a step back and examine what we would do in hypothetical situations. I will challenge the readership to total up the number of yes or no answers to the following questions:

1. You are rushing to meet an appointment. A policeman stops you for not wearing your seat belt. He fines you Le400, 000 to be paid on the spot. You realise he may not pay the money into government coffers and his receipt is probably forged. Would you pay him Le 20,000 knowing he would let you off the hook?

2. A very close relative is about to be sent to prison by the magistrate on a Friday till the next court session on Monday for a crime you are certain he did not commit. A friend suggests he could be granted bail with an under the table payment of Le 300,000 to "persons unknown" and offers to do the deal. Will you give him the money?

3. You want to secure government land and are asked to see an official at the lands ministry. You have been going there for two weeks without success. You finally manage to fix an appointment with the official but he wants you to get him ten gallons fuel to be able to meet you so you can visit the site. Do you give him the money?

My guess is you had a lot more yes than no answers-one yes answer would mean that you are not dissimilar to those who answered the survey in the affirmative. Would not a recent report by the ACC in which they claim that 70% of respondents in a survey claimed the Police was corrupt corroborate the TI survey results generally?

The real concern is why the Government comes out with guns blazing on an issue that is as old as the hills. Simply put, bribery is systemic and we probably consider it a way of life.

I rather prefer the ACC's views to that of the Government in their respective press releases.

The government spokesman was in no mood for a mea culpa in his release-"Government views the recent 2013 Global Corruption Barometer report........as not being statistically representative because the sample size of 1,028 respondents in a population of about six million people, the distribution of the sample population, and the sample frame used remain inadequate... Government is of the firm view that the inconsistencies ...are largely due to sampling errors emanating from a baseless sample frame thereby questioning both the validity and reliability of the results;"

The ACC press release did not condemn the TI but was a rallying call to us all: "While we continue to muster the necessary efforts to deal with bribery in all facets of public life, we would like to call the attention of the general public to the negative and indelible effect of bribery and indeed any other form of corruption, if it is not dealt with aggressively by all and sundry."

The real truth is that our core institutions and basic services are being undermined and the AFP may be a pie in the sky if we do not address these issues. Huguette Labelle, Head of TI summed the situation best when he said: "Too many people are harmed when the core institutions and basic services are undermined by the scourge of corruption". I know Mammy Yeabu in Kurobola was not consulted and I have a sneaking suspicion that apart from Country Lodge, other respondents may have been chosen from STOP PRESS restaurant or the Pavilion restaurant! But, seriously, let's get real. It is time for us to take this systemic issue seriously as a nation.

Ponder my thoughts.

# July 23, 2013

## GLAD TIDINGS ON TRADE FROM IVORY COAST

Many of our compatriots traverse our borders into neighbouring countries to buy their wares and bring them back home for sale. One often wonders why we have to buy goods from Guinea and sell them in stalls here when the products are not even manufactured in Guinea. The rational question to ask is: Are our freight costs or custom duties so prohibitive? To compound the problems, many of such goods are smuggled across the border. Palm oil and other agricultural product are sometimes smuggled across to neighbouring countries often resulting in shortages and price rises.

There is however a noticeable absence of goods actually manufactured in Sierra Leone or neighbouring countries in this cross border trade. Our manufacturing sector is nothing to write home about and most goods manufactured here are sold locally. Kudos, however to companies like Sherkandas which have been relatively successful in exporting to our neighbours.

I was therefore pleased to be one of the representatives of the Sierra Leone Chamber of Commerce, Industry and Agriculture at a working session at the Foreign Affairs Ministry organised by the Mano River Union (MRU) for a group representing the Ministry of African Integration and Ivorians Abroad and members of the Ivorian private sector who visited Sierra Leone to have discussions with the Chamber, amongst other groups on how to increase cross border trade in Mano Union River countries.

Founded in 1973 by Sierra Leone and Liberia, the MRU was joined by Guinea and Ivory Coast in 1980 and 2008 respectively. It covers an area of 754,428 square kilometers with a population of about 45 million, of whom approximately 60% are youths. The sub-region is a huge market with immense market potential but this remains largely untapped. The main objective of the Union, to promote cooperation and economic integration of its four Member States is therefore a laudable one. Trade plays a vital role of in the acceleration of this sub-regional economic integration process.

The intra-Union trade is governed by the Eleventh Protocol on trade which states that:

- No customs duty on imports or similar fees is taxable on all goods of origin from any Member State. (Art. 1);
- No customs duty on imports or similar fees is taxable on any product manufactured by a Union industry (Art. 2)

Industrial products manufactured in the Member States should include at least 35 o/o of domestic components and at least 20% of the company shares should be owned by nationals of the Union Member States for the product to be recognized as originating from the Union.

Since the creation of the Union only two industries have had this status: the-glass factory of Monrovia and fruit juice factory in Freetown.

One would have thought that with these laudable ideals, intra-union trade would be flourishing. One statistic that caught my attention was the fact that trade among member states of the union is very low (around 2%). Constraints faced include low production, insufficiently qualified workforce, and inadequate public infrastructure, weaknesses in energy supply and harassment and extortion (rule of law problems).

The Industrial base of many of these countries is very weak. Industry in Sierra Leone only accounts for 8.4% of our GDP (with manufacturing only 2.4%). Apart from the Brewery, Sherkandas and a few others, we do not make any thing for export. How can we compete with cheap imports from China and India when we generate power at $0.30 per KWh -about three times that of competitors? The West African Power pool has been in the offing for quite a while but its realisation for us may still be distant. How do we work efficiently and compete with a workforce largely untrained and with so many hidden costs of doing business? The roads leading to neighbouring countries are sometimes pitiful. You will realise this on the Sierra Leone side when you attempt to travel to Liberia. As for harassment and extortion, our "men in blue" and their Customs mates do not do us proud. There are at least five checkpoints along the road from Bo to the Jendema border town with Liberia. One optimistic note though- we may not be as bad as some of our neighbours who have more checkpoints and whose Police and Army often ferociously demand bribes. Our guys may be much more civilised and circumspect. They give real meaning to the expression "under the table".

Clearly we must support the development of road infrastructure, improving on the interconnection between member states. The MRU Secretariat says it is also considering the possibility of revitalizing the Airline called Air Mano as well as a Coastal navigation company operating along the coast of the Union Member States within the framework of a partnership between the public and private sectors (their words not mine). The training of our workforce through more and better vocational schools is essential. The WAPP must be speeded up. By far the area in which we can make quick gains is that of harassment and extortion. This greatly adds to the cost of doing business and incurs delays.

Clearly a lot can be done to develop the immense potential of the sub-region by promoting trade in a fully integrated sub-regional market. Congratulations to MRU and to the Ivorians for bringing this issue to the fore and to the latter for having a whole Ministry dealing with African integration.

## REVISED SIERRA LEONE DICTIONARY

A few years ago I wrote an article titled "A new Sierra Leone dictionary". The war had brought a lot of new words or brought new meanings to oft used words. Some of these words like Awareness were due more to the post war harassment of women. "Awareness" referred to "a skin-tight short, in other places worn for athletic purposes but in Sierra Leone worn by women to make rape difficult. Also comes in very handy if you want to make a quick escape from trouble. Handy for women but disliked by "peeping toms" and rapists". Thankfully for our women those days are over-or at least largely over. Others like workshop and stakeholders are still pertinent and stay in the dictionary. There are however new ones which have made their way into our national lingo-many from the political landscape. Ponder some of these in the new edition.

**Workshop**: A gathering of people, to discuss issues related to some development topic. A lot of talking, eating and drinking ending up in revamping old resolutions that are never implemented. This is normally followed up by a decision on the next workshop.

**Sensitisation**: The process of informing the public about something that should be done but is never done.

**Go Police:** An arrogant expression usually by a perpetrator; a euphemism for "go to hell". The recipient may well be advised not to take it too literally and approach the "Men in blue" who would make you wish you had never considered it. Staying put and swearing by Ariogbo or the use of a witch gun may be better ways of seeking redress.

**Project document:** That which is written for the purpose of getting money and for which only partial implementation is meant

**Youth;** Normally those between 15 and 35. Modified now to include the large mass of illiterate, unemployed folk. Wanderers above 35 are also included in this group.

**Committee;** A group of people who get together (for sitting fees) to decide on when to hold the next committee meeting

**Agenda:** Usually refers to an upbeat summon for change and over time could even lead to prosperity. A marked change from the dour Poverty Reduction Strategy Paper references of the Green (peace?) movement of yore. With several more mutations, paradise may not be off the mark.

**College graduate**: Usually refers to someone who has withstood strikes and all kinds of adversity in education including throwing of "number 2" bombs and who upon finishing cannot get a job.

**4 for 4:** Political slogan of the RED movement during their last five yearly fight with the Green (peace?) movement. Recently used by the Greens to disparage the non realisation of expectations. The "women on that street" do not like the change in meaning.

**Board**: A group of political appointees who circumvent all basic rules of corporate governance and resort to showing management teams of companies how to run the company by actually running it for profit (guess who profits?).

**Statistics**: The art of counting people to indicate whether they are progressing, running to stay in the same place or retrogressing. When all of them are counted this results in a census (as long as Mammy Yeabu from Kurubola does not go to the farm on that day!). When a few are counted and the results are good they support the prosperity theory. Would however need to count more people if the results turn out to be bad.

**Paopa (ism)**: Origin unknown, but anecdotal evidence is that it was picked up at sea. Lingo usually crops up after a violent sea wave. Usually refers to a perceived no nonsense "my way or the highway attitude" by the accused. Potentially divisive term in the Green (peace?) movement but liked by the REDS. References to "huen huen" (ask a Mende speaking friend to translate) may serve as an antidote (Understand this at your own peril unless you are part of the Green (peace?) movement)

**Selection:** Election with an S in front. No show of hands necessary as universal brain scan in room can do the job of discerning your choice. Any complaints about the addition of the S could be done quietly later. Used by the reds with the justification that removing the S as the Green (peace?) movement does may result in needless rancour. Whatever the case, do not replace any other letter with an r after you remove the s.

Ponder my dictionary.

Ponder my thoughts.

# July 29, 2013

## "THREE WISE MEN" ON NATIONAL COHESION

I have been particularly struck by articles and speeches by three Sierra Leonean thinkers on the issue of national cohesion as part of the debate on the new constitution. Dr Yusuf Bangura, a renowned political scientist, now retired from the UN has written widely on the political situation in Sierra Leone. Dr Abdulai Conteh is a former attorney general and foreign minister and an international jurist and academic of no mean standing. The third, Dr Omodele (Dele) Jones runs the FJP management consultancy and is not only a Chartered Accountant but holds a doctorate in Business Administration. All these gentlemen have approached the issue of national cohesion from different angles. One common thread that runs across their views is that ethnicity is an extremely serious problem etching away at our brittle national cohesion.

Yusuf Bangura laments the fact that the composition, leadership and electoral base of the two major parties are unequivocally ethno-regional-in the 2012 elections about 80% of the APC's presidential votes came from the North and Western Area. Similarly, the SLPP presidential candidate obtained about 76% of his votes from the Southern and Eastern regions. According to Bangura, "Party activists and sympathisers have developed a sense of entitlement or exclusion, depending on their location in the ethno-regional divide, and perceive politics as a zero-sum game in which losers believe they are excluded from key resources and offices and winners take everything. Losers and their supporters, in turn, tend to discredit most development efforts by the government". Bangura says "It is clear that these provisions (in the constitution) have been insufficient to tame the scourge of ethnic division and antagonism in our politics". His prescriptions would require at least one cabinet minister to be drawn from each of the fourteen electoral districts and various initiatives to de-ethnicise our political system.

Dr. Abdulai Conteh, addressing Sierra Leoneans in Maryland on a whole range of issues opined thus: national cohesion:
"This is the one and extremely important political challenge facing the country: How to forge alliances across regional, ethnic and other divisive forces, including religion, so as to present a cohesive national platform for electoral purposes under the new dispensation. In my view, so much rides on this. Can we individually and collectively rise up to it? I believe we can and should".

Dele Jones approaches things from a totally different perspective. He would give the various regions/ethnic groupings sufficient economic power in the governance system as to result in greater competitiveness to the benefit of the entire nation. The Inclusive National Conversation (TINC) for Constitutional, Economic & Cultural Competitiveness is based on the premise that the unitary model in Africa fails to deliver essential society-building services. By offering "winner-takes-all" rewards, this system accentuates social frictions. He calls for a con-federal state in which each region has adequate economic and decision making power-a marked departure from the current electoral system which concentrates power at the centre.

The President has on many occasions said he takes the issue of national cohesion seriously. Stories however abound of the opposition claiming that his rhetoric has not been matched with action. Abdulai Conteh in his speech says that even with our present system, we could have checks and balances on many issues but that the other arms of government may be giving in too much to the Executive to the extent that a feeling of omnipotence often sets in. According to Conteh "the office (of the President) is without question, one of veneration and honour; and if its occupant sets the pace, tone and example, he can, together with the advice, cooperation and consent of Parliament, provide the leadership that will enable the country to realize its potential for growth and development amid its abundant resources".

One is still concerned that with all the host of special initiatives being undertaken by Government, National Cohesion seems to be given short shrift. The logical offices to which one could conceivably appeal have proved to be quite impotent for alleged cases of discrimination. A major problem might also be that many supporters see a new Government as an avenue for getting plum jobs. The formal private sector is still extremely small and direct government jobs or government influenced ones in parastatals and other government influenced private sector institutions will be the ones most sought after. A long term solution of sorts will be to beef up the potential of the private sector.

The constitution prohibits discrimination on the basis of race, tribe, sex, place of origin, political opinions, colour or creed; and affirms that a political party should not be restricted to only one ethnic group and should not 'advance the interest and welfare' of only one ethnic group, community, geographical area or religious faith. These problems do however exist. There is no singular panacea. The fact that you have these three wise men joining the chorus of compatriots who think this issue should be addressed is what is important. Whilst we grapple with this issue taking the constitutional route, the President may want to consider a special initiative on national cohesion, spearheaded by an interparty/inter regional team of committed Sierra Leoneans who eschew bigotry of any sort. Time for action!

## JZF MEETS CKK: RIP

*Disposer supreme, and Judge of the earth,*
*Who choosest for Thine the weak and the poor;*
*To frail earthen vessels and things of no worth*
*Entrusting Thy riches which aye shall endure.*

*Those vessels soon fail, though full of Thy light,*
*And at Thy decree, are broken and gone;*
*Thence brightly appeareth Thy truth in its might,*
*As through the clouds riven the lightnings have shone.*

I could be excused for using the words of the hymn writer in talking about two "frail earthen vessels" who have done their own little bit to further the practice of journalism in Sierra Leone but are now "broken and gone". Last week, John Zeinu Foray (JZF) was laid to rest. I knew John well through my late brother Christian Katta Keili (CKK), also a journalist in the same radical mould. He often rebelled against Pios, his elder brother just as Christian did with me. They were both lovable non conformists.

Fitting tributes were given at John's funeral by veteran journalists George Koryama and Frank Kposowa, a friend, Dr. Alpha Wurie and on the family side by his son and niece Arabella Foray. A fine pen pusher, a devout Catholic (even attended a 6.30 mass on a visit to Gbinti-according to Alpha Wurie-a Church in Gbinti?), a man who cared deeply about his family, a fearless journalist who pursued the truth and a good investigative journalist with an uncanny sixth sense-these were views from the tributes.

My relationship with JZF had been well cemented with his close relationship with Christian with whom he started his sojourn in the journalism profession. Christian had got me into the newspaper business by happenstance. What started as an assistance to a business venture of a brother got me sucked into helping with the management of the paper. Christian was obviously not pleased that "this Engineer elder brother" was stepping into his turf and thus started a rebellion, with John staunchly in his corner and with the occasional orchestration from the equally radical Oswald Hanciles who was also a columnist and a close friend of Christian's. My "interference" taught me a lot of things about the newspaper industry. My greatest lesson learnt was that I should probably not attempt to understand it. I recall being asked by a journalist in the newsroom; Mr. Keili, should it be "food for thought" or thought for food?" My answer was diplomatic-"It depends on how hungry you are".

I learnt a lot from these two idealistic, free spirited, journalists. They both had a passion for the job. They would both fearlessly endanger themselves to get at the truth-Christian being embedded with the Karmajohs and John pursuing the AFRC and mercilessly beaten in the process. They were good investigative journalists. Both could not be bought over or intimidated. I recall a time when a colleague in high professional circles was pursued by Christian. He came to me with an ultimatum: "get you brother to drop this issue otherwise I will sue him". When I mentioned this to Christian, he showed me stacks of evidence implicating my friend and told me to advise him to keep quiet or else he would reveal even more. I advised my friend to "ride the wave".

Here is an epitaph written for Christian by his friend Abayomi Roberts in 2007.

"One who was a passionate media worker in spite of the huge odds in Sierra Leone including abject poverty and extreme violence towards journalists...? He got more satisfaction from a sold-out edition than the pittance of an allowance/salary we got from management... He was an 'embedded' journalist (in the Sierra Leone rebel war)) long before his counterparts in the West made the term familiar."

Kwame Fitzjohn wrote recently about JZF:

"Pios is the writer. Hindolo found himself in the right place at the right time... But all things considered, it was Jon who was the radical through and through, the real revolutionary that had the vision to take his people to the Promised Land."

In an uncanny way, both statements could apply to either of them, they were both patriotic and brave; proud and playful. Yet, humble and loving. They also loved family.

Let us thank God for the lives of JZF and his friend CKK and hope that the journalism practice will imbibe the positive examples they set for the profession. These frail earthen vessels may have disappeared, but the profession remains full of their light shining though the cloud. Let us thank God for their lives:

Laud and honor to the Father,
laud and honor to the Son,
laud and honor to the Spirit,
ever Three and ever One,
consubstantial, co-eternal,
while unending ages run.

RIP, JZF

Ponder my thoughts

# August 3, 2013

## REFLECTIONS ON RETIREMENT

Last week there were stories in the media about the Ministry of Education retiring over 900 teachers. Apparently, most of them were way past the retirement age; some had conflicting ages reflected in various employee related documents. Verification of teachers has been a big problem with the Ministry and "ghost teachers" seem to be coming out of the woodworks by the day. According to the Minister, some of these teachers were as old as sixty five for a profession that calls for a retirement age of 60-the official government retirement age.

Under normal circumstances, employees would look forward to retirement, especially when they realise that they will enjoy a good rest and a healthy pension. A decade back, the retirement age in Sierra Leone was only 55. In fact during the immediate post-colonial days people retired at an age as low as 45. The raising of the age to 60 was with the realisation that a good many civil servants were being taken out of the workforce in their prime. Thanks to modern medicine, people are generally living longer. In many advanced countries, there are more and more 'old' people compared to people who work, making state pensions harder to fund. Pension funds must be sustainable. If people live longer yet retire earlier, you will not have a large enough base of working people contributing to pensions.

Age 60 is an age at which people still have to offer. One must however be mindful of the fact that there are a great many people who have waited for years to take over the vacancies created by these retirees. The forgery of age in Sierra Leone is much too commonplace. I recall a friend I knew in Tongo who was applying for a job at Rutile which required a sprightly young man. This was around 1985. "What age are you?" I enquired. "Thirty five", he answered, with some uncertainty. I looked at his grey hairs with some incredulity. "When were you born?" I probed."1930", he ventured. "Look here", I said, "you either give me your age and I fix your birthday or give me your birthday and leave the age calculation to me". "Any one sir, a know say you go help me", he replied. There have been stories of ex teachers who had joined the civil service and had their ex schoolboys retire before they did.

This is a serious situation and points to the fact that people can ill afford to retire in Sierra Leone from any form of Government service. It is however a matter of great fortune that Nassit was created by an Act of 2002 by President Kabbah. At least retirees can now look forward to getting some pension, however inadequate it may be. There have however been some fears expressed in various quarters about the future sustainability of the scheme. As with all pension schemes what happens is that as more and more people retire, benefits are increased to keep up with inflation, and as the life expectancies of retirees increase, the cost of meeting this obligation can balloon beyond the scheme's ability.

Our Nassit scheme is well designed and the Act and operational guidelines of the scheme quite robust as to ensure its longevity. Nassit's annual report and audit report are required to be approved by Parliament. Moreover an actuarial review is required by an external consultant every three years. I quote from my last annual Chairman's report in 2007 the conclusion from an actuarial review done the previous year. "The Actuarial review reaffirms the financial viability of the scheme. The scheme can last for another 20 years without requiring an increase in contribution rates if there is no marked adverse deviation from its present path." Government, as guarantor of the scheme and with an overarching obligation for the welfare of workers and their future protection should be concerned about the management of the scheme in all its spheres. It behooves any government to ensure that Nassit is run well for the future of our retirees. Younger people should be doubly concerned as it is they that stand to lose most.

Nassit may be a partial, even if an inadequate solution to the retirement needs of government workers. Large formal private sector companies that pay higher wages will have their workers ending up with larger Nassit retirement payments. Some even augment this with private pension schemes. The great majority of Sierra Leoneans however work in the informal sector and are not subject to the same retirement constraints. They would however need some sort of coverage and it is good that Nassit has a long term view of creating a scheme for the informal sector.

Coming back to government workers, extending the retirement age will merely be a way of prolonging the agony. Evidence abounds that the lifestyle of many government workers drops drastically on retirement and it is tragic to see people slightly over 60 that held high positions of responsibility struggling to make ends meet. This need not be so and there are a few people who are becoming innovative in addressing this problem. I am aware of the case of some civil servants who have done well in the private sector by the dint of their hard work. Some own hotels and guest houses; others have gone into various forms of agriculture-some with spectacular results. Still yet, some have set up consultancies. Come to think of it, a Permanent Secretary in good health retiring at 60 is a big reservoir of knowledge about how government functions and can set up or join a consultancy group. There are a few government teachers who on retirement have found their way into private schools and are still contributing to education. Whilst such people cited are succeeding, the great majority are however struggling and have had to cut back drastically on their lifestyles. Some have met their demise much earlier than they should have.

Perhaps some thought ought to be given by government and private institutions to assisting retirees set up shop in the private sector. This, admittedly is not easy, considering the high unemployment rate of much younger people. Whatever the case, retirees need to prepare a few years ahead of retirement and perhaps create a niche for themselves in the private sector. They also need to realise that whatever the case, they cannot expect to maintain their current life styles. Having successful kids who can provide some "top up" also does help in our kind of social setting. One advice often given is that retirees should begin to offer to serve in the community- the local church, community organisation or other activities. Longevity has a direct relationship with service. Those who serve age gracefully and are not bored. Nassit does help and the government should do all in its power to ensure that the scheme remains solvent to serve our future generations. The government should not allow confidence in the scheme to flounder.

## THE MOBILE PHONE SCOURGE

Anyone old enough to have suffered the indignity of lining up at odd hours at SLET to make an overseas call or generally had the misfortune to have lived through the "land lines only" days will tell you that mobile phones are heaven-sent.

The impact on the effectiveness of organisations, small businesses in various sectors, trading, communications etc. is unimaginable. "How did we do without it?" one is often tempted to ask.

There is however a more murky side to things and though not peculiar to Sierra Leone, we have managed to perfect our own way of doing things. Our culture of dependency has virtually assured that a lot of people in positions of responsibility, others who are the main breadwinners of our extended family system and politicians who incessantly get badgered by constituents or pure harassers do not answer their calls unless they know who is calling and choose to talk to that person. Many have resorted to getting several variations of business and private lines.

I recall a case of a particularly "pious" supporter during my recent political sojourn, who insisted on religiously waking me up at 4 am for "special prayers" much to my wife's chagrin. "Mr Keili, let us pray", he would instruct. Not being one to turn down any special divine favours, I obliged for a few days especially as he seemed genuine and was not asking for any pecuniary inducement. But then on day four, he said: "The special prayers need to be extended to a wider group but I need to buy some special candles, olive oil, torch lights, batteries"-all totalled five hundred thousand Leones. To preserve my sanity, I negotiated for a much lower figure and convinced him that the good Lord will still listen to his supplication at a more hospitable hour and in private.

Some desperate people even go to the extent of using other lines if they suspect you do not want to talk to them. "Ar catch you, so you nor wan talk to me?" as if it is obligatory. Subterfuge has also been quite common. Unguarded snapshots in compromising positions and recording of voices without permission are now commonplace. Have you also noticed that a lot of people you come into contact with "have just dropped their phone by mistake into a bucket of water" or got it stolen? Don't bother to offer to replace them with a Le100, 000 PRSP phone, they will tell you in all probability "Ar wan the one way day snap en get WhatsApp". Don't underestimate how technologically savvy people have become! Not understanding the time difference with the USA, my aunt in Kailahun would complain that her son in the US had adopted his usual habit of sleeping during the day, as she was in the habit of phoning him at 10 am Sierra Leone time.

Whatever the inconvenience, the benefits outweigh the nuisance value. By all means use it but with some circumspection and be aware of the motives of other users. Give me my mobile phone any time!

Ponder my thoughts.

# August 6, 2013

## A NEW CHIEF SHEPHERD FOR THE ANGLICAN CHURCH

"My brother, the people have chosen you and have affirmed their trust in you by acclaiming your election. A Bishop in God's holy Church is called to be one with the apostles in proclaiming Christ's resurrection and interpreting the Gospel and to testify to Christ's sovereignty as Lord of Lords and King of Kings.

You are called to guard the faith, unity and discipline of the Church, to celebrate and to provide for the administration of the sacraments of the New Covenant, to ordain priests and deacons and to join in ordaining Bishops: and to be in all things a faithful pastor and wholesome example for the entire flock of Christ. With your fellow Bishops you will share in the leadership of the Church throughout the world. Your heritage is the faith if patriarchs, prophets, apostles and martyrs and those of every generation who have looked to God in hope. Your joy will be to follow him who came, not to be served, but to serve, and to give his life a ransom for many.

Are you persuaded that God that called you to the office of Bishop?"

To this assertion and concluding question pronounced by the Archbishop and Primate of the Church of the Internal Province of West Africa, the Most Revd. Dr. S. Tilewa Johnson and Lord Bishop of Gambia, the new Anglican Bishop-Elect answered: "I am so persuaded."

Thereafter Thomas Arnold Ikunika Wilson was consecrated as the third Bishop of the Diocese of Freetown. Bishop Wilson J.P, C.O., T.C, C.P.S., B.Th., until recently vicar of the Church of the Holy Trinity Church, Kissy Road, and a man slightly shy of 50 was replacing the recently retired Bishop Julius Lynch who had held the position for the past 17 years. Thomas Wilson had risen from humble beginnings, the son of a carpenter father and a seamstress mother to make it to the pinnacle of the Anglican Church. He had been a school teacher, a Sunday school teacher, youth fellowship member and a Catechist before joining the priesthood twenty years ago and had served in several churches in the Diocese and on several of its important committees.

The impressive ceremony at the Cathedral Church of St. George on August 4, 2013 was superintended by a host of bishops from the other dioceses in the province who assisted the archbishop. The Archbishop based his text on John 21:16 the charge to Peter; "He saith to him again the second time, Simon, son of Jonas, lovest thou me? He saith unto him, Yea Lord, thou knowest that I love thee. He saith unto him. Feed my sheep." He reminded him about the obligations of being a Bishop as espoused in 1 Tim 3:2-7-onerous obligations to which he should endeavour to adhere. The Lord will provide for him, he continued-"When God calls, God equips". In his typical humorous fashion the Archbishop described himself as a midwife, who was delivering a new baby for the diocese assisted by nurses: the bishops. He admonished the local church that he would expect to meet a healthy bouncing baby when he comes back after sometime — not one with kwashiorkor.

Bishop Wilson faces a monumental task in leading this historic church. He will be attempting to follow in the footsteps of fourteen illustrious bishops who had headed this church since May 1852 when the former Diocese of Sierra Leone was founded. This includes Dr. M.N.C.O Scott of Sierra Leone who later became Archbishop of West Africa, the first African archbishop. The Anglican Church has been in the vanguard of education. The Church founded the Grammar School and Annie Walsh and played a leading role in the early formative years of Fourah Bay College and was once the "Official State Church". It is now however faced with immense challenges. The Anglican Church like many traditional churches has undergone a sustained period of atrophy with the members taking off in droves for Pentecostal Churches. It could certainly do a lot more to improve the lot of its priests and manage its not immodest real estate holdings. The new bishop will be faced with a considerable number of challenges and some would say the Church has to "reform or die".

The Anglican Church in Sierra Leone is still in many ways inherently conservative just like its mother Church was, as expressed by Mathew Arnold in 1877 who described the Church of England (Anglican Church) as "an institution devoted above all to the landed gentry, but also to the propertied and satisfied classes generally; favouring immobility, preaching sub-mission and reserving transformation in general for the other side of the grave"

Mathew Arnold may have been very harsh, but in many ways this description may not be way off the mark for today's traditional Churches that do not want to change. In many traditional churches "Christians have largely neglected what it means to be a disciples of Jesus Christ and have just become church-members, pew-fillers, hymn-singers and sermon-tasters" according to one critic.

Bishop Wilson can avert this apocalyptic situation with his leadership and our prayer for him is that he will be the sort of servant leader who will engender the required change. The Worldwide Anglican Church has considerable latitude in its liturgy and the ways services are conduced and even in interpreting its doctrines.

The hope of many Anglicans is that Bishop Wilson will take up his cross with humility. He should however not be daunted by the weight of office as he should trust that the Lord will give him strength. These two verses of the hymn "Take up thy cross" would be apt for him to ponder.

Take up thy cross, the Savior said,
if thou wouldst my disciple be;
deny thyself, the world forsake,
and humbly follow after me.

Take up thy cross, let not its weight
fill thy weak spirit with alarm;
his strength shall bear thy spirit up,
and brace thy heart and nerve thine arm.

As Anglicans our prayer for him is that the Lord pitches his tent with him, so that he may not become deterred by hardship, strangeness and doubt; that he may show him the movement he must make toward a wealth not dependent on possessions, toward a wisdom not based on books, toward a strength not bolstered by might, toward a God not confined to heaven.

**FINALLY, SIERRA SCORES HIGH!**

One set of statistics that we all agree with (even Mammy Yeabu in Korobula) is that relating to religious tolerance. We could definitely top any comparative table for countries. A Muslim marrying a Christian is now much too commonplace. There is nothing wrong with having a Christian wedding followed by a Muslim one or vice versa. A quick check in Pentecostal churches in town will reveal a good number of Muslims, especially women who find the message appealing and regularly attend Church.

Many of us have been beneficiaries of this cozy relationship between Christians and Muslims. I certainly have. I recall with fondness my Muslim uncle, Bobor Komi at Upper MacRobert Street, Bo whom my brother and I visited during the fasting period. With his food (sunakati) stacked on a table and him praying close by, we were hungry and got impatient with his rituals. We started helping ourselves to the meal on the table. He noticed from one corner of the eye that the food was disappearing fast. He put his prayers on "acceleration" with the bowing and rising at an unusually high fast and furious pace until the prayers ended (prematurely in our view). This was followed by a wave of the finger and a stern rebuke to lay off his food.

Our village could at one time boast of having an equal number of Muslims and Christians. The 6.00 am call of the minaret was matched by the early morning Church bell. The level of cooperation within various denominations is also improving. It was good to have the Catholic Archbishop Tamba Charles bless the family of Bishop Lynch during his valedictory service. Many Muslims who attended Christian schools know many favourite Christian hymns by heart-you might just be out gunned by a Muslim Harfordian in singing Church hymns-they know them all by heart. One critic has opined on this that he wished they had taken the other subjects as seriously-needless to say I don't subscribe to this!

A politician would normally ensure he knows both the Lord's Prayer and the Al-fatia by heart-not surprising for people who speak from both sides of the mouth! The SLPP Presidential candidate and running mate at the last election spent considerable time visiting Churches and Mosques not only for divine intervention but for meeting people. Nearly all formal national occasions now start with Christian and Muslim prayers. It is inconceivable now for a major political party in Sierra Leone not to balance the ticket, religious-wise. This has been the case for all major parties in recent elections, with the usual suspicion of potential candidates changing their religion.

An oft misunderstood statistic is that related to beer consumption. The Brewery claims that beer sales plummet during the fasting period. One could almost safely jump to the conclusion that you have a lot of Muslim beer drinkers who abstain during the Holy month. I will not be tempted to commit such sacrilege during this holy period and much prefer the explanation given by a Muslim friend who says, "The Christians who normally drink alcohol with their soft drink gulping Muslim friends decide to stay away from the bar as an expression of solidarity with their Muslim friends." How nice and convenient!

We should be pleased that we are in a country that has such religious tolerance. One wonders then why this tolerance cannot be translated into ethnic and tribal tolerance.

Ponder my thoughts

# August 13, 2013

## LESSONS FROM KING JIMMY BRIDGE

The accident at King Jimmy Bridge has received wide attention. Our condolences to our unfortunate compatriots who lost their lives in this unfortunate debacle and may the souls of those deceased rest in perfect peace.

I did visit the site over the weekend. Excavators were still removing rubble and bystanders reckoned there may still be more people caught under the rubble. Some displaced residents living in the vicinity of the bridge still had their bundles of whatever they could scavenge of their property close by. The bridge itself was a high mound of cobblestones aggregated together with concrete and paved atop to bridge the natural valley. It had two large culverts beneath and seemed at first glance like a solidly built structure that had gone into a state of repair. On either side of the bridge, almost underneath it were some old shacks that had housed people. There were still shanty house precariously close to the bridge and with appurtenances blocking whatever drainage there was. Vestiges of stalls that had been perched by the side of the bridge with some elements supported by the bridge could still be seen.

The human pressure on the bridge and its support was all too apparent. This neglect of bridges and roads is much too commonplace. A few months ago we witnessed the problem with the Mabang Bridge and there have been complaints about the state of many other bridges. The bridge at Pyke Street has been mentioned as another prime candidate. Buildings of all sorts exist underneath the bridge at Adesanyah Street. The list goes on. Many of the main roads of Freetown are in a state of disrepair and have been made worse by the rainy season. The fact remains that we have always as a nation neglected basic maintenance of our roads and bridges-in fact all infrastructure.

We are always more impressed with new things. Road maintenance is politically unattractive – new road construction is more "visible" and produces greater political prestige hence the temptation is much too strong for any government to put an inordinate amount of attention on new roads and neglect old ones. Maintenance does not have the same status or does not give the same opportunity to stakeholders or decision makers to present themselves to the public. Politically, a new toad sells better than perching old roads. Even for the professionals, working with maintenance is still looked upon as a low status occupation. Yet even small budgets for maintenance make a difference with proper planning and the right priorities. The money which is saved in the maintenance budget by not maintaining the roads, is ultimately paid by the users and the society. It is often forgotten that building of roads is only a part of the total transport cost. While this total cost includes maintenance and building costs, it also includes the full cost of running vehicles on a road, an expense that climbs rapidly as the surface starts to deteriorate. As a road gets busier, maintenance costs increase. A new road is expensive and a two lane paved road could cost as much about 0.6 million US dollars per Kilometre on an average. Routine maintenance of such a road could cost about 10,000 US dollars per year per Kilometre. If the maintenance is neglected, it will cost five or six times as much to restore the road. Economically, it is an indefensible waste.

Many countries therefore have alternative, more regular sources for road maintenance, less vulnerable for competition from other public sectors. One way to do this is to introduce road users charge, as the fuel levy and to create an autonomous Road Fund. Many African countries like Zambia and Tanzania have established such a Road Fund. Sierra Leone has also done this but there are problems between the Road Maintenance Fund (RMF) and the SLRA and funds for maintenance are always under threat, especially if a government artificially forgoes revenue from fuel levies to keep prices down or if the funds are not well apportioned.

Another important point of note in this debacle is the poor planning of Freetown and the ineffectiveness of state Ministries, Institutions and the City Council in addressing the planning problems of Freetown. An interesting book edited by Christopher Fyfe and Eldred Jones-"Freetown-a symposium", published in 1968 indicates this is not a new problem. In it Milton Harvey and John Dewdney, writing about the planning problems in Freetown state that the major problems are future expansion of the city, intra city mobility, inadequacy of services and unemployment and crime. The population of Freetown in 1792 was 100 and in 1963 it was 127,917-it is now ten times the 1963 figure. In 1939 there was a report of a slum clearance committee which had interesting solutions. The conclusion of the report was "Too many opportunities have been lost already because of the lack of any planning. Unless it is soon available uncontrolled growth will continue and the urban problem will become progressively more serious and difficult of solution". S.R. Dixon Fyle, in the same book, writing on the social problems of Freetown gave the following opinion: "This issue of enforcement and compliance had several dimensions. It was for instance a political problem in which certain categories of citizens conferred on themselves and, by proxy on their associates, a virtually impenetrable immunity from formal accountability."

These observations even in the "good old days" of the 1960's could only get worse in 2013, with a tenfold increase in the population of Freetown. The planning problems of Freetown still continue unabated. The Ministry of Works, Housing and Infrastructure (MOWHI) is inter alia in charge of the construction, reconstruction and rehabilitation and overall maintenance of the road sector infrastructure. The Ministry also gives out building permits. The SLRA plans, develops, maintains and administers the trunk roads and related facilities. The Ministry of Lands, Country Planning and the Environment is in charge of land allocation. The City Council has responsibility of street trading. All of them to some extent have a say in such issues. It is interesting that everyone at this stage seems to be "passing the buck". The squatters and street traders haven't come out of this exactly smelling of roses. Also, there has been some finger pointing at NPA and Sierratel — those perennial whipping boys for digging up the road. On the flip side, some "residents" say they had warned (do not know exactly who) that the bridge was giving way. I even learnt over the radio that there were two organised clubs for the "bridge residents"-"T Unit" and "Pressure Clean". Whatever the case, there is a seedbed of confusion at the moment. The same comments on bridge safety could equally apply to building safety. Half way up Hill cot Road, one could see a multi storey building about 200 yards off the road, sliced in half, crumbling on top of a neighbour's house-luckily there were no fatalities.

The Sierra Leone Institution of Engineers (SLIE) has been concerned about the uncontrolled development activities within the City. SLIE particularly cited structures at Moa Wharf, Genet Wharf and at the back of Sierratel complex. According to its advisory note to Government, SLIE stated: "It is very disturbing to know that most of these buildings are constructed without proper planning permits. Council therefore recommends that: 1.A temporary ban is imposed on private development along the hillsides........ And along the sea-face of the coastline etc. 2. A broad based committee be formed comprising representatives from the Ministries of Works, Technical Maintenance and Infrastructure, Lands Country Planning and the Environment, the SLRA and representatives from SLIA (Sierra Leone Institution of Architects) and SLIE to deliberate and advise in this area.3. That the statutory laws of the land should be fully invoked to correct and arrest this chaotic situation."

Budgeting for an immediate inspection and remedial action (however temporary) of major bridge structures may be in place. It is obvious that addressing such problems requires an inter-ministerial/institutional approach and most of all the political will to make what may be considered unpalatable decisions. Planning laws must be obeyed and political considerations should in no way be allowed to hold sway. As Dixon Fyle wryly noted "The "free" in Freetown and the heritage of liberation bred an atmosphere of casualness and bluff which lay at the back of many of our problems." Many would argue that the "free" still exists in "Free" town.

## THE ROAD CONSTRUCTION INCONVE-NIENCE CONTINUES

The advantages of new roads projects cannot be disputed and any well meaning citizen would welcome a well conceived and executed road project. No one should be unreasonable to expect that these projects cannot proceed without some inconvenience to users. The cavalier attitude of some construction companies is however worrisome. As mentioned before in this column many people have gone without electricity and water for prolonged periods because of this as cables and pipes are moved for unduly long periods. This needs better liaison between the road construction companies and the utility companies. What is however irritating is that road companies do not even bother to put up signs for some road diversions. Drivers have been forced to get themselves into corners sometimes with unwelcome results. Hazardous areas like gaping holes are not even marked and one could keep going round in circles in you cannot discern the correct detour. Surely with a little bit of thought these problems can be sorted out. It is no excuse to say they are so busy with the construction that cannot be bothered with "small matters". These are not mundane-they can save lives and obviate unnecessary inconvenience. Time to get tough!

Ponder my thoughts

# August 21, 2013

## LAWLESSNESS AND INDISCIPLINE IN OUR MIDST

Lawlessness is fast becoming the hallmark of our society. Indiscipline continues to mar our political landscape, threatening out national unity and hard earned democracy.

Examples abound of the economic costs of lawlessness in many sectors. In the educational sector the lack of discipline, which interferes with the teaching and learning process, manifests itself in various ways including bullying, vandalism, alcohol and substance abuse, and truancy which translate into poor academic output. Cheating is rife in exams and teachers compromise themselves in so many ways. We ultimately end of with ill educated youth who leave school and can contribute very little to the workforce and society in general.

In the lands sector, land planning is poor and there is general indiscipline in the land market. Enforcement of laws is generally very poor and planning is almost absent. Illegal buildings and structures abound in many areas. The transport sector does not fare any better. Taxi and poda poda drivers and Okada riders drive and park with abandon. There have been recent stories of a good percentage of Okada riders not being licenced. In a recent case in the North, two policemen were beaten by a group of Okada riders when they arrested two of them for riding unlicensed bikes.

The effect of poor sanitation, poor garbage collection, illegal acts like throwing garbage with abandon anywhere, practices that create stagnant pools of water are very telling on the health of the populace and consequently on our health expenditure.

I listened with a bit of sympathy to the lamentations of the beleaguered new Mayor of Freetown who complained that it is very difficult to implement bylaws of the city council and law breakers were let off either by the police or with a mere slap on the wrist by the judiciary. He wanted the arrest and detention powers of the Metropolitan Police to be strengthened.

In nearly all parts of the country, there is damage to infrastructure. From the people who cut electric poles and wires and steal transformer oil from NPA transformers, to those who damage bridge railings, lawlessness is all too apparent. Vandalism in our politics has become much too commonplace.

Legal recourse has often not been a solution as it has been much too slow and ineffective. Some efforts have been made by the Attitudinal and Behavioural Change secretariat, civil society and various groups to sensitise people and engender change in people in various spheres of society but it would seem that these messages have in the main fallen on stony ground. It is clear that a considerable effort is needed to change out national psyche o the issue of lawlessness.

Our society should be one
• In which human rights are respected
• In which the individual's dignity and worth are acknowledged
• In which the rule of law is observed
• In which people willingly fulfil their responsibilities, and
• In which the common good is the concern of all.

Effective civic education programs should provide us with many opportunities for the development of desirable traits of public and private character. Character traits such as civility, courage, self-discipline, respect for others, punctuality, personal responsibility can be fostered in school and community service learning projects. It is however apparent that one cannot leave this to civic education alone. It must be accompanied by enforcement with stiff punitive measures in many instances. Legal and enforcement issues however pose severe problems. If, as seems to be the case, public enforcement agencies like the police, lands officials etc. do not meet the standards required by the citizenry, the public is likely to start breaking the law and find excuses for dishonesty.

The case of Singapore may provide some indication on how we should proceed on this issue. A blogger writing on Singapore states:
"This is one of the few places where you can walk around the city at all hours of the night without being harassed, mugged or in fear of your life...There is also no graffiti, no vandalism, and a much higher degree of respect for people than anywhere else I have lived... Sometimes what is required in a highly civilised society is draconian measures. In Singapore the importation and sale of chewing gum is an offence and people can be prosecuted and fined significant sums for dropping litter, smoking in public places, or failing to flush a public toilet after use."

Others may say it is easier for Singapore and other Asian countries because Asian values are typically described as embodying the Confucian ideals of respect for authority, hard work, thrift, and the belief that the community is more important than the individual. The real question is what are our Sierra Leonean values? Not surprisingly some of these values have also been with us in Sierra Leone. In our traditional settings we have always had respect for authority and the rule of law and even hard work. These values have however changed over time-the war and its social ills it has wrought including youth unemployment have certainly not helped the situation.

We can perhaps in trying to address this conundrum listen to the sage advice of the architect of Singapore, the legendary Lee Kuan Yew, in his book "From third world to first". "They laughed at us (referring to foreign journalists who derided him for running a "nanny state"). But I was confident we would have the last laugh. We would be a grosser, ruder, cruder society had we not made these efforts to persuade our people to change their ways. We did not measure up as a cultivated, civilised society and were not ashamed to set about trying to become one in the shortest time possible. First we educated and exhorted our people. After we had persuaded and won over a majority, we legislated to punish the wilful minority. It has made Singapore a more pleasant place to live in. If this is the "nanny state," I am proud to have formed one."

We may also have to move from education and legislate and enforce to punish the wilful lawbreakers.

## SLPP CONVENTION: RIGHT MESSAGE, WRONG MESSENGERS?

My young niece had a jibe at me after the SLPP convention. "Ponder my thoughts", she called me disparagingly, "I dare you to write about your SLPP convention". Well, I am writing this piece just so she could lose her bet, even though I had long resolved to keep internal party politics out of my column for the main reason that I believe this is best handled within a party. Also, it may be unfair to use the bully pulpit of a newspaper column to pontificate about what should be done in the internal workings of a party.

Having declared that opening salvo, I will report on the recent convention in Bo by mainly talking about what happened on the fringes, with the advice given to the SLPP by two likeable but some would say cunning characters-Alpha Kanu, Minister of Information and Publicity Secretary of the APC and Mohamed Bangura, leader of the UDM. Alpha Kanu was dressed in a long green gown and a red cap-embodying the colours of the SLPP and APC. He had entered the hall a few minutes before he was asked to speak. According to him, he was a bit late because he had been waiting for his tailor to finish sewing his green gown as he had none in his wardrobe. He mentioned that he had almost joined SLPP in his younger days as he was in fact an errand boy for his SLPP uncle who had sent him by bicycle many a time on party related matters. He advised the SLPP to participate meaningfully in the current constitutional review process. The erstwhile Chairman John Benjamin donated a green cap to him to match his green gown, as he was leaving. He stressed the need for inclusiveness and lamented the problems of the SLPP. They should take a leaf out of APC's book and be united, he advised.

Mohamed Bangura mentioned the fact that of nine political leaders in the country, he was the only one gracing the occasion. He had had his quarrels with SLPP especially with John Benjamin but had put all of this behind him now. He was embarrassed at the infighting in the SLPP. The presence of police and army was not as a result of the machinations of the APC but because of the internal party conflict. The SLPP needed unity and if they did not have it they would be relegated to third position (of course UDM would be second), he warned. The SLPP also needs to extend its influence beyond the south and east of the country in order to be a truly national party. My first reaction to this lecture was "Oh, how has the mighty SLPP fallen, to be lectured on unity and decorum by APC and UDM!"

Now, back to the convention itself. My personal view is that all the fun has been taken out of the normal convention. In past conventions, people could be seen holding their banners to support candidates or tout a particular district or organisation. Beer and food stalls flourished and there was generally a gay and happy mood. Thanks mainly to our internal problems, there were so many manned police posts and we were frisked extensively before entering the hall.

An object lesson to be learnt from all of this is that SLPP must guard the "N". I will elaborate. During the days of the train, there was a sign at the train station in Segbwema for Njaluahun Secondary School for girls with their motto "Forward ever, backward never" emblazoned. Some mischievous person was in the habit of removing the "n" and putting it in the wrong place so that it became "Forward Never, backward ever". Thereafter,

Njaluahun girls jealously guarded their "N" by installing a watchman to guard it. SLPP must do the same-guard its "N".

Ponder my thoughts

# August 27, 2013

## SCHOOL ALUMNI ASSOCIATIONS: UNSUNG HEROES

A recent newspaper story reported that the CKC Old Boys Association (COBA) in North America had sent furniture and equipment to their alma mater that included chairs, desks and computers to the tune of $50,000. The National President of COBA, John Bosco Kaikai revealed that the donation was in preparation for the forthcoming Diamond Jubilee celebrations of the school which will commence by the end of this year. Meanwhile, a ten classroom building will be constructed as part of preparations for the school's pending Golden Jubilee celebrations. The Old Edwardians Association recently launched a school building project aimed at increasing the school's seating capacity in readiness for the one shift school system recommended by the Gbamanja Commission. The school presently has over 2000 pupils. The same story continues with nearly all major schools. The old students' associations are trying to outdo each other in assisting their schools in myriad ways.

The principal objective of an alumni association is to form a bond of union between Old students and the school to promote the maintenance of their interest in the School and their willingness to assist in its welfare, and to promote the ideals for which the school was founded.

Our current education crisis carries high costs. It is consigning a whole generation of Sierra Leonean children and youth to a future of poverty, insecurity and unemployment. It is also starving organisations of the skills that are the life-blood of enterprise and innovation and undermining prospects for sustained economic growth. The critical challenges in our secondary schools includes limited infrastructure, limited learning and teaching materials, low morale and productivity of teachers, limited technical facilities amongst others. All of these mean poor pass rates in public examinations and poor quality of education generally.

The intervention of alumni associations is mainly geared toward addressing such problems. Some Associations like the Sierra Leone Grammar School's have gone the route of partially privatizing the school with spectacular results. Alumni Associations are building classrooms, instituting revolving salary funds for teachers, giving incentives for high performing students and teachers, supplying equipment, equipping school labs and libraries-nearly the whole works. Some have representatives on Boards of Governors even though the Ministry of Education is not compelled to appoint representatives from alumni associations.

All the major schools have alumni associations. They range from Kenema Old Students Association (KOSA) to the famous Old Bo Boys Association (OBBA), to the Prince of Wales and Annie Walsh to St. Francis in Makeni-a good geographical spread. Over time I have seen old students who are so overzealous about their schools that for them, Old student's functions and annual gatherings are de-rigueur. I recall at Sierra Rutile, the Harford Old Girls Association (HOGA), whose members we fondly referred to as HOGS (note-not in a piggish way) had a membership of five for an association with eight positions in the Executive. They solved the problem by doubling up on jobs! You can't help but note the fervour with which OBBA members look forward to their annual gathering in Bo over the Easter weekend (doubtful though if it is just for the school!). Governments and individuals know better than to mess around with successful alumni associations of long established schools-the cases of the misappropriation of the Grammar school land and the "Annie Walsh market" saga are all too fresh in our consciousness. Even the newer or less well known schools are playing catch up. There was a recent story about the Deputy Internal Affairs Minister, Sheka Tarawalie and his classmate

SLBC Director General, Gbanabom Hallowell launching the Old Birch Students Association at the Wesleyan school's complex in Makeni City where the school held its first Speech Day and Prize giving ceremony.

These associations certainly have influence both collectively and by the individual dint of some of its members. Some alumni associations include many notable personalities, including heads of state, politicians, academicians, scientists, doctors, lawyers, engineers, educators, architects, diplomats, computer scientists, agriculturists, accountants, artists, business leaders and industrialists. These people are scattered all over the world and look to their schools with nostalgia. Major Sierra Leonean schools have a large core of illustrious old students. Perhaps none can however match Achimota School in Ghana, a co-educational boarding school located at Achimota in Accra, Ghana. The school, founded in 1924, has educated many African leaders, including Kwame Nkrumah, Edward Akufo-Addo, Jerry John Rawlings, and John Evans Atta Mills all of whom are former Heads of State of Ghana. The current President of Ghana, John Dramani Mahama, is also an alumnus of Achimota School. Former Prime Minister Dr. Kofi Abrefa Busia taught at Achimota. Also included in its list of African heads of state are Zimbabwe president Robert Mugabe and Sir Dawda Jawara, first head of state of The Gambia. Impressive indeed!

One can imagine what such illustrious old students can do through their alumni associations. President Koroma's influence on a hitherto moribund Magburaka Old Boys Association (MOBA) is palpable. Their annual gathering in Magburaka even attracts a host of "old boys" who never darkened the walls of that institution. Sir Milton Margai and Siaka Stevens at Albert Academy and Sir Albert Margai and Ahmed Tejan Kabbah at Edwards probably gave some impetus to their alumni associations. Alumni associations have also done a yeoman's job for national unity and cohesion and for cutting across the stratified social status of its individual membership and create that special bond between old students on the "right hand side of the normal age distribution curve" and young students who represent the next generation. They also cut across the political divide (except perhaps for our unfortunate COBA-with our illustrious Old Boys, Berewa and Margai). There is so much to write about this, but we will leave this for another day.

Our schools are certainly in dire need of help. Just yesterday, I heard over the radio that the famous Prince of Wales School received no subvention from the education Ministry and the only funds received were school fees which were grossly inadequate to meet the school's expenses. The Old Boys Association was helping to pay the salaries of some teachers who had not been approved by the Ministry, building a new school block and shoring up the coastal defence system as the school's infrastructure was threatened by water incursion due to encroachment on the school land.

Sierra Leone cannot build economic success on failing education systems. Development assistance levels for education has stagnated and the education sector continues to attract limited interest. Government's educational budget is inadequate and the Ministry remains severely challenged in meeting its mandate. Government should perhaps cherish the role of these alumni associations a lot more and formalise the Ministry's relationships with alumni associations. Duty free concessions, tax breaks, participation in Boards etc., should be considered and existing initiatives improved upon. The Ministry may want to consider getting their views through some sort of collective advisory body. It will be unfortunate if the enthusiasm demonstrated by these associations is dampened. Kudos to our unsung heroes who help prop up our failing schools.

## A BRIGHT LIGHT IN THE JUDICIARY

I looked at the headline of a recent newspaper column and saw the words "Human Rights Organisation" and "Judiciary" and almost expected the story was about some confrontation. To my surprise, a civil society organization, Humanist Watch Sierra Leone (HW-SL), had awarded the Acting Principal Magistrate in Kenema, Alhaji Mohamed Momoh-Jah Stevens "for his diligent role in the dispensation of justice in that part of the country." National Coordinator for HW-SL, Titus Masallay said they were very happy with the manner in which the magistrate handles cases, especially those relating to abuse of young girls and women and Sexual and Gender Base Violence (SGBV) in the district. Mr. Masallay said the magistrate has always stood firm in dealing with such cases despite numerous challenges faced in eradicating the ugly act. The Magistrate was being transferred to another region.

Without an independent institution responsible for administering justice, a culture of human rights cannot prevail. When the independence and integrity of the judiciary is compromised the citizen is left at the mercy of a system which does not guarantee protection against the offences of power by the state. Ultimately citizens' trust in the democratic institutions of the state rely on the knowledge that if need be, they are entitled to a fair trial; recognised by all major human rights treaties as a fundamental, non-disputable right.

Several criticisms have been levied against our justice system by the public at large and human rights organisations. The huge delays in the courts culminating in several years of case backlogs, keeping suspects in remand for an unduly long period of time and accusations of corruption and collusion in the justice system are much too commonplace. This overall has resulted in lack of trust in the justice system. Thanks to several initiatives undertaken under the auspices of several donor-led and government projects, change may be in the offing in certain areas. Although the beefing up of the capacity of the Law Officers Department, the Fast Track Commercial Court and a few other developments should be lauded, our judicial system overall is still threatening to break at the seams.

The lack of trust by the public and human rights organisations in the judiciary is tangible. All the more reason why people like Magistrate Momoh-Jah Steven should be lauded for his performance. Not everyone can be honoured on the annual National Honours lists or by groups like AWOL. However when one is honoured by organisations within his locality for services rendered to the society, he should be justly proud. It is hard to live with integrity in a society where desirable qualities are constantly violated. Trying to live with integrity can leave one feeling isolated. Magistrate Jah has not ignored, squelched, quenched or seared that inner voice urging the right. He has been dependable, doing his duty and living up to his responsibilities. Congratulations to Magistrate Stevens! By the way, is he a COBA member?

Ponder my thoughts

# September 10, 2013

## KING JIMMY: NOBODY DID WHAT ANYBODY COULD HAVE DONE

This is a story of four people named **Everybody**, **Somebody**, **Anybody** and **Nobody**. There was an important job to be done and **everybody** was sure **somebody** would do it. **Anybody** could have done it but **nobody** did it. **Somebody** got angry with that because it was **Everybody**'s job. **Everybody** thought **anybody** could do it but **nobody** realized that **everybody** wouldn't do it. It ended that **everybody** blamed **somebody** when **nobody** did what **anybody** could have done. To this date these four people are still arguing why **nobody** did the job.

This familiar quip reminds me of the King Jimmy Bridge saga. I was invited by the BBC Media Trust to be a panelist on the weekly Fo-Rod programme last week on bridge safety. The BBC Media Trust airs its programmes over thirty radio stations nationwide. I believe I was supposed to be an honest broker. What was my "claim to fame"? I had written about the collapse of the bridge in this column a few weeks back. I am glad I did accept the invitation as this was indeed an eye opener for me.

Here is a summary of the views from the various groups represented.

*PARLIAMENTARY OVERSIGHT COMMITTEE ON WORKS (Represented by Hon. Kombo Kamara)*

- Concerned that Ministry of Works was not represented even though invited.
- SLRA had very little to show for the recent Le 52 billion funding and other funds from Road Maintenance Fund.
- SLRA doing a poor job of checking bridges and general performance leaves a lot to be desired

## KING JIMMY MARKET SELLERS ASSOCIATION
*(Represented by Chairlady. Also other views from group)*

- Knew bridge would collapse. Had in fact informed City Council about possible impending disaster
- King Jimmy market is renowned market centre. Business severely affected because of bridge collapse and many traders cannot even meet gbara (debt) repayments.
- Bridge had nearly collapsed before but was patched. Should have been condemned and new one built.
- Old PWD is much better than SLRA. Not satisfied with SLRA's performance.
- Association should be asked for advice on construction of new bridge

## BBC MEDIA TRUST *(airing of Vox-pop on bridges round the country)*

- Gbere bridge is in a poor state...broken components, footpath damaged...people fall inside water, railings broken.
- Mabang Bridge in a state of disrepair. Le1, 000 to cross river by boat with an additional Le1000 per bag of rice.

## SLRA *(Represented by Director of bridges and Assistant)*

- Bridge was checked this year and is checked every year. Did not anticipate failure. Water volume this year high. Have not ascertained reason for failure.
- SLRA often faces financial problems to fund maintenance programme
- Axle load restrictions being flouted on bridges-mining companies affected Gbere Bridge and big trailers affected Mabang Bridge.
- New bridge to be constructed at Mabang and Gbere through donor funding.

- PWD not better than SLRA-Changing circumstances as PWD had some 4000 km of road to manage whereas SLRA has 11,000.
- New bridge to be constructed at King Jimmy

*ANDREW KEILI*
- Unfair to only target SLRA as much as they may be culpable. Other players-SLRTA, Utility Companies, bridge community, Road Maintenance Fund should also be questioned
- SLRA needs to improve on PR as public unaware of any maintenance programmes or successes scored in programmes.

*POSTCRIPT*-All groups save me, lay the blame for the bridge's collapse squarely at SLRA's doorstep. SLRA boxed defensively but never got out of its corner to land any punches. I suspected they could not, probably out of deference lash out at the Works Ministry or the Road Maintenance Fund or indeed point to any culpability by the Freetown City Council, market traders, bridge residents or other agencies. It was also clear that SLRA needs to improve on its PR to inform people about their successes and any limitations not of their own making. There seems to be no authoritative answer to why the bridge failed. It would also seem that members of the public have now become "bridge inspectors". There is also some confusion as to what the right reporting channels should be, should anything untoward be noticed.

In all probability, the bridge, made of cobblestone cemented together may have been affected by flooding. Most bridge failures happen during floods. Flooding can collapse bridges in a far more insidious way -- by gradually wearing away the earth around and underneath the bridge piers. This process is known as scour.

SLRA is obviously been pilloried for the collapse of the King Jimmy Bridge as well as the problems with other bridges. There are a few questions however that one would like to ask other groups to get a holistic picture of things. May be after we get honest answers we would be inclined to conclude nobody has done what anybody could have done. Here are the questions.

*Freetown City Council*
1. Were you informed about problems with the bridge? If so, what did you do about it?
2. Did you by yourself or through any Ministry or Agency attempt to move the bridge residents?

*SLRTA*
1. How do you physically regulate the use of bridges by vehicles which exceed axle load limitations for bridges? Do you display such signs?

*SLRA*
1. Have you ever provided your work programme and progress of maintenance work on bridges and status of bridges to your Parliamentary Oversight Committee or Works Ministry?
2. Do you keep an inventory of all bridges showing current status and red alert warnings?

*Road Maintenance Fund*
1. Same questions as for SLRA
2. What percentage of requested maintenance jobs by SLRA can you conveniently fund?

*Ministry of Works*
1. Same questions as for SLRA
2. Why can't the public be adequately warned about dangerous bridges and other dangerous situations with infrastructure?

*Parliamentary oversight Committee on Works*
1. Same questions as for SLRA

*Bridge Residents*
1. Would you be willing to vacate you present premises in the interest of safety? Under what conditions?

*King Jimmy Market Traders' Association*
1. Would you be willing to vacate you present premises in the interest of safety? Under what conditions?

BBC Media Trust did a swell job-congratulations to them. It is obvious however that there are still more questions than answers. Somebody has to do what nobody seems to want to do and instead blames everybody else.

## MENDE WOMEN ARE BEAUTIFUL!

Time was, when there were hardly any beauty salons in this country. The situation has changed markedly over the last two decades and hairdressing salons are all over the place. Even our local male barbers are now ensconced in beauty salons-after some initial trepidation I now feel at home sitting side by side with a largely female clientele at Kornya's on Brook Street when I go for my haircut.

Salons come with varying levels of sophistication but the end result is that our women folk spend a lot of time and money in doing their hair in a multiplicity of styles. Whether it is by relaxing the hair, attaching various types of natural or artificial hair to their own hair, dyeing the hair in a multiplicity of shades or braiding in different styles, the end result is that our women truly enhance their natural beauty. OK, you do have the odd outrageous hairdos that would do "Janet Bundle" proud (Oh, by the way "Janet Bundle" was a mad woman with an outrageous hairstyle in Kenema when I was growing up). The great majority of our womenfolk have become truly stunning. Throw in the pedicure, manicure and all the other "cures" and our men folk are put in mortal danger, just crossing the street.

Move over, modern Sierra Leonean women! All of this is not new. Mende women have something to teach us about the hair beautification process. I have been reading about it in Mariane Ferme's book, the Underneath of things (violence, history, and the everyday in Sierra Leone). She had stayed as a Peace Corps volunteer in Kpuawala Village in the Wonde Chiefdom Bo District, She quotes from Aldridge's book of 1902 thus:

"The longest operation is the hairdressing, which may take some days. A woman may be seen lying on the ground with her head in the lap of the operator. who after combing out the wool with a native wooden comb, with little prongs, joins on other pieces of wool that are most elaborately plaited, and continually added to until the required height is obtained. There are numerous designs in this hairdressing, and.... it is quite a science, the most common and favourite pattern rather suggesting that curious cell-like concretions known to geologists as the brain stone, the top being embellished by a little silver or leather gree-gree."

Marianne herself describes hairdressing with the Mende women she encountered: "Each new hairstyling session was an opportunity to experiment with new designs, many of which acquired names and were associated with events surrounding their introduction to the area. When travelling to market or encountering female visitors from urban areas, women were attentive to their hairstyles and studied them in order to reproduce them at home.......women often said that finely braided hair was one of the key elements in seducing men."

No wonder Mende are so beautiful. Oh, and Temne Women and Limba women and Loko women, and..... All Sierra Leonean women are beautiful!

Ponder my thoughts.

# September 17, 2013

## NATIONAL ASSETS COMMISSION: AWOKO CHASING SHADOWS

The Chairman of the National Assets and Government Property Commission, Alhaji Unisa Sesay aka Awoko has recently been up in arms against some civil servants over the way and manner he says they misuse government property.

The National Assets and Government Property Commission Act of 1990 is "an Act to establish a national assets and Government property Commission and a national register to make provision for the control and identification of all national assets and Government property to provide for their maintenance and improvement of such property and to monitor their use and disposal and for connected purposes." Whatever may be entailed in this "legalese", it has certainly not been an easy task for the avuncular Awoko who has got himself in a spin chasing Government assets in every nook and cranny.

The Commission has been largely irrelevant since its formation and has faced major challenges over the years related to non compliance by various Ministries, Departments and Agencies (MDAs), occupation by illegal occupants of Government buildings and the seeming lack of political will to address the problem. Illegal squatters occupy many old government buildings and the government seems incapable of moving them. My friend Awoko himself, as PRO of the Chamber of Commerce has been chased before by a group of disabled illegal residents as he tried to retrieve a building handed over by Government to the Chamber. Only a Hussein Bolt-like dash for dear life saved him.

According to Awoko, no MDA should dispose of Government property without prior notice to the Commission. Many a

Government property is now in the hands of third parties. The Commission faces capacity constraints; it has inadequate logistics and personnel and does not even have regional offices. Without an assets register, the Commission is unaware of the existence of many properties owned by Government. The Commission is certainly aware of the rampant encroachment on government property but is hampered in addressing the problem.

Government assets and properties are varied and primarily within the purview of so many MDAs that the Commission finds it difficult merely keeping up with developments. These range from Government office buildings, government quarters, assets of institutions such as SALHOC-including the OAU Villas, recreational areas, machinery, office equipment and furniture and property owned by moribund institutions such as the Sierra Leone Railway, SLPMB etc. Some of the assets like those belonging to the SLPMB could be transferred to new institutions as was recently the case.

Maintenance of buildings is a serious problem. Government owned buildings are falling apart. There is hardly any maintenance done on any facilities. We had to ask the Chinese to help us refurbish the Youyi building and the National stadium. We cannot even maintain our infrastructural facilities, let alone cater for any expansion.  Most Ministries have not got the capacity or even remotely the level of funding to cope with these problems. Unpainted buildings, broken window panes, and unkempt surroundings are the order of the day. Worn tiles, doors that are permanently closed or permanently open, non functioning ventilators, electrical fuses and switchgear that have been damaged- the list is endless.

Government does apportion some money for periodic maintenance but this is pitiful. The situation has been exacerbated by years of neglect, causing maintenance costs to spiral out of control. Government apart, the occupants are also another matter. The gross misuse of government facilities is common. The proliferation of food sellers, hawkers, hustlers in these buildings subject facilities to unusual usage rates. The normal occupants indulge in their own share of the abuse.

Boarding a lift in Government buildings is not for the fainthearted. Permanent lift attendants are the order of the day. No point looking at the lit up numbers as often they do not coincide with the floors for some strange reason. To the quizzical some explanation by the beleaguered attendant may sometimes be necessary. "The third floor is now actually the fourth floor." Or "This lift does not stop at the sixth floor-you would have to go up to the seventh floor and come down the stairs to the sixth."

The rampant misuse of government vehicles is much too commonplace. There have been instances in which government vehicles and mobile equipment have been left abandoned for want of some minor part. Left abandoned, parts are sometimes cannibalised or stolen until the equipment becomes totally obsolescent. Government vehicles are subjected to gross misuse for non government related functions.

Maintenance problems and misuse notwithstanding, policies related to Government assets and property remain uncertain. The fate of SALHOC and the management of the OAU Villas remain uncertain. It is alleged that Government properties have been illegally appropriated for private use by major functionaries of Government. Government land is within the purview of the Lands Ministry-that is quite another story. The fate of many properties confiscated by Government over the years is shrouded in secrecy or controversy.

It is into this seedbed of confusion that Awoko and his commission have walked-it is an uncertain walk! He has however been bold enough to cite some defaulters over the media but he himself admits that a lot of the shenanigans might be perpetrated with the connivance of senior government functionaries and politicians. The best Awoko can do at the moment is to rant and rave and probably embarrass top people who may be defaulters. It however begs the larger question of accountability. With most assets belonging to individual MDAs, such assets can be accounted for through their normal accountability systems, if these work. MDAs also do a lot of purchasing for all kinds of items-Furniture, electronic equipment etc. which should remain state property.

Despite the difficulties of addressing this problem at a national level, it is heartening to see something being done about it with Local Councils. The Public Financial Management Reform Unit [PFMRU] in the Ministry of Finance and Economic Development, in collaboration with the National Assets Commission recently reviewed the draft fixed Assets Policy for Local Councils. The basic goal and objective of this policy is to define and describe a set of standard procedures and policies necessary to record and control the changes in fixed asset system of Local Councils in accordance with generally accepted accounting principles. This policy is also geared towards providing guidance on how to deal with capital expenditure and the purchase and disposal of fixed assets.

The million dollar question then is: If this is being done for Local Councils, why can we not ensure it is done properly at the national level?  Also, what changes in maintenance policy does the Ministry of Works, Housing and Infrastructure, responsible for maintenance of Government buildings intend to adopt to ensure better maintenance of these facilities? What is the current policy on the allocation, use and disposal of Government quarters and the land surrounding these quarters? What is the future of SALHOC, the OAU Villas and other Government housing projects? What is the general policy of disposing of other buildings owned by Government? Is government property being sold in secret? When is the Commission going to have a register of Government assets? Without addressing these sorts of questions and sorting out grey areas in responsibilities of MDAs

as related to government property and assets and the
Commission, things are not going to work out and Awoko and
his Commission will continue chasing shadows. Time for action.

## PRODUCTIVITY? WHAT PRODUCTIVITY?

I was pleasantly surprised at some honest statements made
recently by the Chinese Ambassador to a group of journalists on
the issue of productivity in Sierra Leone. After the normal
platitudes of cooperation, shared vision etc. and praising us for
our more recent positive political strides, he was blunt about our
productivity-or rather the lack thereof. Simply put, we needed to
have a more positive attitude to work and inculcate values such
as keeping to time. Our work ethic has to improve.

I cannot argue with his Excellency's sentiments. I seem to lose
count of how many public holidays we have. On Fridays,
Christians and Muslims would absent themselves from the
offices. To avoid revellers who want to enjoy themselves at other
people's expense, workers absent themselves from work, move
away from the office or barricade themselves inside the office. I
recall when at Rutile, an American Engineer Colleague
complained to me about what he thought was the aggressiveness
of one worker who told him "Rick, this year, you will pull my
Christmas, ma".

Turning up for work late and leaving work much too early are
the order of the day. Interject this with time taken off for our
many social events including weddings and funerals and the time
taken off work adds up significantly. Come December, we have
the carnivals and other parties. I've often wondered how many
hours a year the typical Sierra Leonean worker spends at work.

And what happens at work? Relentless phone calls make
unavailable hours total up. Then comes the attitude problem.
One has seen workers in Government offices watching Nigerian
films at work. The really ingenious ones kill their immediate

relatives many times during their lifetime of work. This reminds me of this story I heard last week at my Dinner Club. A boss called a worker and asked him: "Do you believe in life after death?" "Yes, I am a Christian, I do, and he answered." "Good for you, said the boss, your Uncle whose funeral you attended yesterday called yesterday afternoon and left this letter for you. He may have started his second life too soon!" A friend of mine told me recently that whenever a worker reports a family death and request time off, he religiously records it in his file. He tells me of the case of one cleaner who has killed the same father five times.

A change in culture is required. The motivation, commitment, dedication and willingness to work, absent with our workers must be rekindled. Hard work, tenacity, honesty and tolerance must be imbibed by our workers if we are to improve on productivity in this country. Thank you Mr Ambassador.

Ponder my thoughts.

# September 24, 2013

## CHAMBER OF COMMERCE ON ALTERNATIVE DISPUTE RESOLUTION

*"If your brother sins against you, go and tell him his fault, between you and him alone. If he listens to you, you have gained your brother. But if he does not listen, take one or two others along with you, that every charge may be established by the evidence of two or three witnesses. If he refuses to listen to them, tell it to the church. And if he refuses to listen even to the church, let him be to you as a Gentile and a tax collector." -Matthew 18:15-17*

No, I am not preaching! These verses are Jesus' guidelines for dispute resolution in the Church. They are designed to reconcile those who disagree so that all Christians can live in harmony. In many ways this sage advice may also apply to disputes in business dealings. Many a dispute in business can be sorted out by mediation or arbitration without resorting to lengthy and expensive court proceedings. Disputes are as old as the hills and are bound to occur in businesses dealings in both the formal and informal sectors. The Sierra Leone Chamber of Commerce, Industry and Agriculture on Monday this week launched the initial training programme for Alternative Dispute Resolution organised by its newly established Centre for Alternative Dispute Resolution (CADR).

CADR was established by the Chamber in March, 2010; it was designed to offer Alternative Dispute Resolution methods to its members and the wider national and regional business community seeking ADR services. In many ways, some businesses in Sierra Leone have traditionally utilised ADR to resolve commercial disputes. Many businesses particularly those in the agricultural and petty trading/informal sectors shy away from resolving their disputes through the formal court process. Many communities, including the Lebanese have established their own internal dispute resolution methods. The CADR was established to meet the objectives of ensuring greater transparency in national dispute resolution methods thereby creating an enabling environment for businesses to grow and investors to be confident. It also provides a faster and cheaper process for conducting and concluding commercial disputes using arbitration.

The Business community has welcomed the Fast Track Commercial Court which is greatly assisting in accelerating the resolution of cases that hitherto would take an inordinately long time to resolve through the normal court system. The rules of this court however require a prior attempt to resolve cases through some ADR process before attempting to bring it to court. It is reckoned that the adoption of ADR on a wider scale would reduce corruption in commercial case settlements through the empowering of businesses to 'run' their cases at the CADR.

Chamber has sought international partnership with the Chartered Institute of Arbitrators ("CIArb") which sent trainers to run courses in introduction to ADR and Arbitration and the Accelerated course in arbitration for national lawyers.

Although Sierra Leone has an arbitration Act (the arbitration Act Cap 25) it needs to be replaced. At the launching ceremony at the Bank complex, the Guest speaker who launched the programme, Ombudsman Justice Edmund Cowan, the President of The General Legal Council, Lawyer Yada Williams were enthused about this initiative and were of the view that it would positively complement current initiatives to settle commercial disputes through the court system. Jeffery Alkinson of the CIArb, the course coordinator, a past President of the Chartered Institute mentioned that the institute had a membership of 13000 in 104 countries and has 26 branches. Its work is meant to promote peace and harmony as well as promote international business. The UN's UNCITRAL Model Law on International Commercial Arbitration formulated in 1985 has been accepted in 77 jurisdictions and he was hoping Sierra Leone would be the 78th. Justice Cowan, Lawyer Yada Williams and Chamber Vice

President Christo Forster were confident it would help the private sector. The initial course has been oversubscribed with about 70 participants from various professions, although most are lawyers.

This initiative was the brainchild of the erstwhile President of Chamber, Tunde Cole, M.D of NP and has been nurtured by Millicent Hamilton Hazeley, CEO of Class Consult who runs the CADR Office for Chamber at her 8 Barthust Street Office.

My experience tells me this will be really be useful for the private sector and I could see it especially being useful for the mining sector of which I am more intimately familiar. Mines have peculiar problems related to land, environmental problems, employment of locals, provision of infrastructure, community development etc. One only needs to listen to the morning radio shows to know about the extent of the problems. The recent cases involving the Bollori haulage contract for London Mining and last year's insurrection at African Minerals are as fresh in our minds as are incessant complaints about mining companies by NGOs.

These are not surprising to me. The legal and regulatory framework for the mining sector often lacks specificity, leaving interpretation to be determined on a case by case basis, often by the involved stakeholders themselves. Also Laws pertaining to the sector are diffused across statutes emanating from various ministries, leading to problems of consistency and poorly defined responsibilities. To compound the problem, monitoring of mines is often poor and implementation of laws and regulations is consistently weak. On the flip side some mining companies may complain that the Government cannot wholly abrogate its social responsibilities in mining communities to them and that the expectations from some communities may be unduly high.

It is therefore essential that there is a dispute resolution mechanism that is satisfactory to all parties in order to avoid resorting to the general legal system as much as possible. Such a mechanism would not only save a great amount of time and money; it would also help level the playing field as local community members will generally not have the resources to 'go to battle' against large mining companies in the more formal legal system. Given its relatively low cost, the use of an independent mediator as the first stop in dispute resolution is becoming a very popular option around the world. Arbitration is an alternative to the formal judiciary. It creates a healthy competition to the formal legal system and would not be financially onerous to access for ordinary citizens and local communities.

Certainly the same may apply to other sectors. Kudos to Chamber for this laudable initiative. As more and more people are trained in ADR and hopefully a new Act is promulgated to bring us in line with contemporary ADR practices, we are going to see greater confidence in investing in this country and greater confidence that disputes between various parties can be amicably resolved without expensive and lengthy legal action.

## MOHAMED BANGURA: OPPOSITION LEADER

*Politics hates a vacuum. If it isn't filled with hope, someone will fill it with fear*-Naomi Klein

Many politically neutral people have been lamenting the fact that the opposition is lackluster. They would like to see Government on its toes but the government seems to be marching like an imperial army undeterred by feeble "bows and arrows" thrown at them by a fleeing enemy. As in nature however, politics does not allow a vacuum. Whilst the SLPP is embroiled in internecine warfare, the UDM leader Mohamed Bangura has been engaging the press about the pitfalls of the current Government. His criticisms have swung like a yo yo from the problems of the educational system to conflict of interest issues by Government Ministers, to sycophancy of Ministers, to poor roads-the whole works, As if that was not enough, he has also been espousing his views on the constitution.

Reaction by the public to the newly converted "Paul of Tarsus" has been mixed, judging from the phone text messages from listeners. A sizable proportion of them are suspicious of his motives as he was an ardent supporter of the President and his Government. He still holds the President in reverence and thinks he is the best thing since sliced bread, but lambasts those around him who he calls sycophants. There are also those who praise him for "pressing the right button". They praise what they consider his honest assessment of the country's problem.

Whatever the case he would seem to be the official opposition these days. He is joined by a potpourri of players in the press and civil society who mete out their own share of criticism.
A healthy opposition is essential for the sound working of democracy. The opposition must be vigilant- constantly being on the alert and watchful of the government's policies and actions. When there are well informed critics ever ready to expose the wrongs committed by the government and bring to light its acts of omission and commission, the ruling party can hardly afford to be slack and negligent.

Whatever one may think of Mr Bangura. He seems to be the official opposition these days, albeit a one man bandwagon. His ability to exploit what he considers the problems of government and the resonation of his views with the public cannot however be underestimated. One ray of hope though is that despite all its internal problems, optimists within the party are confident the SLPP will put paid to its problems and ultimately achieve unity. They cite APC's protracted problems before the 2007 elections. Until then, Mr Bangura's vigilance and participation must be applauded, even if temporarily until, notes one cynic "things fall apart"

Ponder my thoughts

# October 8, 2013

## GOVERMENT BY ULTIMATUM

An interesting phenomenon has reared its ugly head in our governance system recently, as civil society organisations issue ultimatum after ultimatum to the Government. It has culminated in the issuance of a press release from the Office of the President reminding civil society of "who is in charge of the nation's affairs".

The press release reaffirmed that Government has a primordial responsibility to seek the interest of the people: "No single organisation or group of organisations can pretend to be seeking the interest of the people more than the elected government which has initiated and is leading the implementation of these programmes." It accused Civil society of being mischievous:"The approach taken by the said civil society organisations is mischievous and a form of moral blackmail which will not be tolerated by government."

Strangely the release says the Government will keep the public updated on the activities cited, though it assumes in a sort of supercilious way that there is nothing amiss: "Government wishes to inform the general public that the respective ministries, departments and agencies will soon be providing the nation with updates on their activities in the specific areas mentioned herein, giving assurances in each case that implementation is on track."

Though the Government only refers to the ultimatums in a few choice areas, the list over the past few months has been lengthy. Here are a few:

The civil society group Health Alert recently gave a three month ultimatum to the Works Minister to address the problem of the numerous potholes in Freetown within three months. The threat?-He should resign if this is not done.

The Association of Journalists on Mining and Extractives, African Socialist Movement, Indigenous Transport Owners Association and Campaign for Just Mining demanded that the haulage contract between Bollore and London Mining be terminated, a direct contract be signed between indigenous transport owners and London Mining and the ACC investigates the entire matter. The threat?-"If all these demands are not adhered to within the next twenty-one days, we will commence legal proceedings in the courts of Sierra Leone to establish the illegitimacy of the haulage contract arrangement in question,"

Members of the African Revolution Sports Journalists Association (ARSJA) gave the Government through the Ministry of Sports a seven-day ultimatum to clear six 20 feet containers of sports equipment lodged at the Quay beginning on August 19, 2013.The threat? - "If no decisive action is taken within this stipulated seven days ultimatum, we shall be forced to take another line of action."

The Sierra Leone Bike Riders Union gave a 21-day ultimatum to the Government to resolve the growing problem between the Union and the Sierra Leone Police due to an incident that occurred at Up Gun, Freetown, on 22nd March resulting in a confrontation between the two parties.

The UDM, not to be outdone has issued weekly ultimatums on all sorts of issues through its leader Mohamed Bangura.

The astute political observer would not however be surprised that we have got to this stage. The various players that have the responsibility of monitoring and evaluating the performance of various MDAs may have in fact been negligent in the execution of their duties. This includes but is not limited to Parliament, through its various oversight committees, the Open Government Initiative (OGI), the performance monitoring unit in the Office of the Chief of staff and technical M&E teams. In many instances, reports from some of these groups have been at variance with views aired by the public over the multiplicity of media outlets. I recently wrote in this column about the senseless spin in the Citizens Report Card issued by the OGI which is supposed to give an indication on what the populace thinks about the Government's delivery of public services. I cited part of the report that made the ridiculous statement that in Kailahun and Kono which have no grid electricity, between 55% and 73% of respondents said they had electricity more than once a week! Who is fooling who?

Civil society organisations (CSOs) have become important actors for delivery of social services and implementation of other development programmes, as a complement to government. They have been very dynamic and advocated for many issues pertinent to our national life. The world over, Social Accountability approaches to effective public service delivery and poverty reduction are beginning to be recognized by citizens and governments as a valid means for improving the efficient delivery of services, ensuring transparency in governance. Even in this country we have seen genuine involvement of civil society in budget formulation and analysis, expenditure monitoring, tracking, and in a limited way participatory performance monitoring of public service delivery. Could the new angst be due to lack of dialogue with civil society on these issues and the feeling by them that the government is whitewashing issues?

The Government's response has unfortunately been both heavy handed and ridiculous. One sympathetic government paper stated- "The decision of the so called Health Civil Society was not done in the interest of the public but is one that smacks of a personal and political witch-hunt." The same paper had a ridiculous postulate-"The way and manner our roads are being used could be one of the major reasons for the potholes. The plying of heavy duty trailers and excavators owned by mining companies could also be a leading factor of potholes in the country. How many times for God sake have these potholes been filled up? Don't you think the more the roads are being used the more we expect potholes?" Indeed a case of excuses gone awry!

Whilst we have national institutions like the OGI going to ridiculous lengths to tout the performance of government, other monitors have been more forthright. In its 2012 report, the African Peer Review Mechanism (APRM) by which a country voluntarily subjects itself to a review by peers in the areas of democracy and political governance; economic governance and management; corporate governance as well as socio-economic development lists down amongst Sierra Leone's constraints to development at the economic level to include: serious lack of capacity, poor monitoring and evaluation process and the key challenges at the social and cultural levels to include poor energy supply, poverty and inadequate and poorly maintained infrastructure. The APRM advised that an effective communication strategy should be formulated for keeping citizens fully informed about challenges, development options, policy content and intended outcomes.

CSOs may overstep the mark from time to time, but whatever their deficiencies they are good for our nascent democracy. Government M&E groups like OGI and Parliament should put their house in order and Government should be less preoccupied with needless spin. As I opined in the article on the Citizens report card "Tinkering with a report to show the Government in a positive light is a disservice to the Government itself and certainly does not give the President the correct picture. This is one spin that has gone too far in my opinion".

Truth be said, the ultimatums by Civil society are fairly innocuous and are not even accompanied by any defined actions that would be taken if their demands are not met except for the London Mining-Bollore one in which they threaten legal action-nothing wrong with this in a democratic society. There is a sense of foreboding in these threats-the government should realize that people demand performance and if not forthcoming, credible answers to their concerns. Governing by titillation may result in government by ultimatum!

## BONTHE: THE FORGOTTEN ISLAND

Bonthe Island has been in the news over these past few weeks for all the wrong reasons. Usually regarded as a far flung out place, this island has been the butt of many jokes relating to the transfer of Civil servants. The story is told of a traffic Policeman who did not "comply" with his boss's wishes in sharing his "collection", being transferred to Bonthe. He wept uncontrollably- Bonthe only had one vehicle! He could have probably done better nowadays with the okadas.

Bonthe Island has a rich heritage. This 19th century British control post against the slave trade in time grew as a shipping port for piassava and other agricultural products. The silting up of the estuary, coastal swamps, and new internal routes have reduced its importance as a port. It is today a caricature of its former self, with its major landmarks lying in ruins due to neglect by successive administrations.

Recent news from the island is worrying. Bonthe hospital is poorly managed and has not even got a doctor. The fish storage project funded by FAO and GIZ is fast becoming a white elephant. According to the Mayor, Bonthe's local fishing industry is in the doldrums because of the recent declaration of the Sherbro River as a Marine Protected Area (MPA). According to Awoko, the Mayor disclosed that people were leaving the island in droves.

Water availability is a problem and the island is flood prone and susceptible to severe sanitation problems. The municipal council finds it very difficult to raise funds. Bonthe also has no electricity. With Government offices and NGOs preferring to be located in mainland Mattru Jong, Bonthe Island continues to be neglected.

One silver lining though-the teacher is King! I listened to a story on FM 98.1 in which a market woman stated that poverty was rife and that teachers were the only credit worthy clients, even though they would not be paid for months. It was Ok to credit them as long as the head teacher stood as guarantor.

The problem of Bonthe is serious. It behoves Government to undertake some special initiatives to restore the dignity and historical relevance of this island. Bonthe descendants arise!

Ponder my thoughts

## October 10, 2013

## STONE MINING: IT'S A DANGEROUS FAMILY AFFAIR

There have been recent embarrassing stories about Sierra Leonean kids as young as three years old making a living from mining stones. One vivid one on YouTube shows children breaking stones to earn enough money for their school fees, studying on candlelight in a squalid room. Thousands of children in Sierra Leone are working as rock-breakers for the country's construction industry. A recent story "The rock mining children in Sierra Leone have not found peace" in the Atlantic refers to this phenomenon as "one of Sierra Leone's post war contradictions". Many of these children do not attend school. The story of Foday Mansaray, a former mobile-phone salesman who set up a school in 2007 in Adonis, outside Freetown in a bid to get children out of the quarries is therefore encouraging. The newspaper story reports "the severely under-funded Borbor Pain Charity School of Hope currently has 380 students, all of whom have worked as stone-breakers, but Mansaray estimates there are up to 3,000 more children engaged in the practice throughout the country."

Stone mining portends more problems however than child labour alone. Colonies of migrant gravel miners live in crude zinc-walled shanties on the peninsular hillsides overlooking coastal Adonkia, Angola Town, and Lakka. The mining involves large numbers of people grouped into 'family gangs' at each site. The operation involves stripping the area of all vegetation and soil cover until bed rock is exposed-soil is dug out around the rock outcrop exposing it. The exposed rock is sometimes heated with open fire fuelled with used tyres or dry tree trunks, making the rock easier to break. Large chunks of rock are broken off the outcrop manually, with a sledge hammer. These are then broken into aggregate of different sizes to meet user requirements. The aggregate is heaped into piles and sold by head pan measurements.

Whole families may be involved in the operation. The men do the heavier work of breaking the large boulders and women and children help break them down to smaller sizes. The mining families earn very little out of the exercise and intermediaries and truck drivers make a lot more money. It is also not uncommon for people building houses to engage gangs of stone breakers to operate within their land and sell the broken stones to the house owner.

Most of these activities have negative impacts on the environment. Mining on the hill slopes creates frequent landslides and rock falls are reported during the rainy season, sometimes with fatal consequences. Extraction locations include ridges, hills, rocky beaches and river beds. The clearing of the vegetation cover for aggregate mining has a high degrading effect on the land. The slopes, mostly steep, become very vulnerable to erosion. Gullies created could cause flooding in down slope areas during the rains. When mining takes place in the sea there is the danger of sea incursion resulting from excavation of rocks as does occur in Bololo in Goderich, while river stone mining could hamper river activities. In the provinces, lowland artisanal aggregate mining is confined to rocky river beds such as that of the Sewa River. Stones are intensively mined during the dry season on the bed of the Sewa River.

There are severe occupational health and safety issues as well as socio-economic problems to contend with. A recent newspaper story reports that an 8-year-old girl, fell and broke her arm at the elbow a year ago. Although set by a doctor, the bone healed at an odd angle and is permanently deformed. Breaking stones could result in hand or leg injuries as well as possible injuries to the eyes because of flying rocks, as well as dust inhalation problems. A study with which I was involved a few years back indicated about 74% of the miners for the York Rural District and 53%

for the Provincial Districts have no formal education. There are no proper toilet and waste disposal facilities within the settlements.

It is glaringly obvious that a web of problems is created ranging from child mining to environmental and socio-economic problems. Stone mining problems cannot be addressed without addressing the wider livelihood problem. Children should be taken off stone mining and given a chance to be educated. The objective of whatever measures that are put in place will be to ensure that the rights of the miners are protected to either continue with their means of livelihood in a sustainable way while discouraging the indiscriminate and non-regulatory method of extraction, or provide an alternative means of living.

Here are a few suggestions that could be adopted in a bid to address this intransigent problem.

- The Government should have a policy on sand and aggregate mining because of their unbridled mining with concomitant effects on the environment and the socio-economic life of affected communities.
- Child labour in the operations should be outlawed. Opportunities should however be provided to encourage the education of children of mining families
- Artisanal rock excavation should probably be restricted to designated sites such as old abandoned quarries.
- Government should put structures in place to monitor these operations
- Artisanal extractors should be required to obtain licences and obligated to mine in locations assigned to them by the appropriate government authority.
- The Government and NGOs should actively encourage the pursuit of alternative means of livelihood in these areas.
- Miners should be encouraged to have umbrella organisations which will make it easier for

government/NGOs to carry out information dissemination on a whole host of issue including safety.

These problems need to be addressed, especially those of the children. As noted by one observer quoted in the Atlantic article "If you let these children go down astray, the country will go astray." But we should not forget-it's a family affair.

## WHAT IF OUR GOVERNMENT SHUTS DOWN?

I am intrigued by the US Government shutdown and have wondered what will happen if our own government were to shut down. A shutdown can happen when a legislative body (including the legislative power of veto by the Executive) cannot agree on a budget financing of the government programs for a pending fiscal year. In the absence of appropriated funds, the government discontinues providing non-essential services. In the US government shutdown, the government stops providing all but "essential" services. Essential or "excepted" functions commonly include those necessary for national security, protection of life and property, and making benefit payments under entitlement programs.

Going by the American definition, some may argue that although we may not have the same political aggro as them, we in fact always have a partial shutdown as the government is always ill pressed to provide funds anyway for both essential and non-essential services.

Let us probe further to find out what may actually happen if we were to have a government shutdown by examining the work of various Ministries, Agencies and areas of work.

**Immigration Department**: If this is shutdown, passports will not be issued out. This may actually be the best way to prevent our passports from getting into the hands of unsavoury characters who tarnish our image overseas.

**National parks and zoos**: In the US, these would be closed for a while to the public. A shutdown in Sierra Leone would probably make people ask about the location of these facilities. Where are our national parks? Is the museum still located by the Cotton Tree?

**Police and Fire force**: Whatever the case, they will be allowed to work. In the US they will not be paid while the shutdown lasts but will have back pay after the shutdown. This could actually be tried with little consequence here. All the Police have to do is set up more illegal checkpoints, ask drivers for "legitimate donations" for once and temporarily keep the money for arrests made for seatbelts. The Fire force could use this opportunity to find out where hydrants are located.

**Parliamentarians:** The Speaker of Parliament has complained that a considerable number of Parliamentarians are absenting themselves from Parliament. A shutdown would only lengthen their "holidays" and who knows-more time spent with their constituents-if home is where they go, may not be such a bad thing. And oh, there will be no danger of bad laws or agreements being passed for a while.

**The President and his Ministers:** I suppose they will still go to work but with government workers given time off they may as well decide to stay at home. Overseas travel may be finally curtailed. There will be no Presidential or Vice Presidential convoys and traffic will be freed up in the mornings.

**Garbage collection:** There will be no money appropriated to the City Council for clearing garbage and it will continue piling up (funds will only slightly be less than at present)- the Public may not notice the difference however.

**Postal service**: The U.S. Postal Service works through shutdowns. We could have our postal service run during a shutdown. They could be made to deliver anything except letters!

**Teachers**: Schools may be shutdown if teachers are not paid. "Ghost" teachers may finally legitimately come out of hiding.
**Health workers**: Our assiduous health workers will continue providing service. Who knows- the missing Doctor in the Bonthe Hospital may even show up!

**The opposition**: They will continue being in the MIA category- Missing in Action and probably arguing about who connived with the Government to cause the shutdown.

OK, but seriously speaking I'm glad we are unlikely to officially shut down. We may be hard to restart!

Ponder my thoughts.

# October 16, 2013

## THE LOCAL CONTENT CONUNDRUM

Local content issues have recently been brought to the fore in discussions on national issues. The Bollore saga relating to the haulage of London Mining's ore and other employment issues, especially by mining companies are constantly in the news. Civil society organisations, local entrepreneurs, organisations of drivers, landowners are all up in arms about this issue , urging that Sierra Leoneans be given priority in one foreign owned business or another. Views have by no means been uniform on the issues. As is often the case, relevant  MDAs have been discordant and sometimes played the populist card. A policy "whose time has come" has been invoked by everyone-some for genuine reasons and others for mainly parochial reasons. It behooves one to take a closer looking at this policy and how it should be implemented.

The local content policy was established in May 2012 for good reasons. The figure for utilization of local supplies in Sierra Leone is alarming for some sectors. According to a recent study, it varies from 0.1% in the oil & gas sector to 5.8% in mining and 45.6% in banking. There are many practical things the Government can do to redress this situation. An examination of manpower planning in Sierra Leone indicates some absurd facts.

1. Despite the fact that Sierra Leone's infrastructure statistics are grim, Engineers who qualify in various disciplines from FBC and cannot get relevant jobs.
2. Mining contributed as much as 20% of GDP and 80 % of export earnings in the 80s and early 90s but our mining companies have had to rely mainly on expatriate engineers.
3. There is no major Sierra Leonean road construction firm even though there are several Sierra Leonean engineers with relevant experience to staff such ventures.

4. Our pool of graduates from University graduating every year is several orders of magnitude greater than jobs that are available to absorb them. Those leaving technical and vocational institutions do not fare any better.

There is often a gross lack of knowledge about the benefits of increased local participation. The local private sector is sometimes blamed for not being proactive enough. Many think a Local content policy borders on protectionism that will not allow us to develop a competitive private sector that can hold its own in the global economy. A good number believes that monitoring and enforcement measures by Government Departments of the implementation of local content legislation will introduce undesirable delays, costs, uncertainties, and unpredictably in doing business in Sierra Leone.

The participation of local companies is now a requirement for many projects funded by donors and the government. Government employment laws relating to preferential employment of suitable locals and the need for skills training and technology transfer to locals are surprisingly sound, but unlike a lot of African countries, these are treated with levity in Sierra Leone. Even though we have our labour laws (our work permit system gives preference to Sierra Leoneans), we are more interested in collecting revenue for NRA from payments made for Work permits. A gradualist approach to address the problems of capacity limitations by a combination of training, funding and other provisions will go a long way towards providing a sustainable solution to this conundrum.

Some local companies, though competent are hampered by lack of capital to expand and improve on the services they provide. Another factor militating against greater local participation is the dearth of technical skills amongst middle level technicians. Our vocational schools are of an inadequate standard to meet the demands of industry. There is very little emphasis put in our educational system towards skills training. The criticism that

Sierra Leonean companies like to go it alone and not pool their resources together may be true to a certain extent but I am certain that if the Government were to actively go out and engender training and encouragement in creating mergers, this will be helpful. Such a system is also bound to work better in an environment where the legal framework is conducive.

A few good things have happened with following through on the policy. The Ministry of Trade and Industry (MTI), as the lead Ministry spearheading the Local content drive has been making the right noises. One is however concerned that several Ministries need to cooperate with the MTI. In dealing with specific industries, the host Ministry and the Ministry of Labour may also be involved. Other Ministries may also be involved. The multiplicity of players at the local level and local businessmen may all have concerns. Expectations may have to be managed. The investor may also have legitimate concerns and may want to run its operations in an unbridled way as long as the company keeps to local legislation and regulations.

DFID as a major sponsor and MTI seem to appreciate the complexity of the problem. A recent advert posted by DFID for assistance to the MTI defines the objectives of the local content very well.

*"The policy promotes the growth of the private sector by creating linkages with foreign direct investments through increased use of Sierra Leonean local content. Specifically the policy gives measures to promote the use of local sourced goods and services, to promote domestic small and medium enterprises through targeted private and government procurement, to encourage employment and training of Sierra Leoneans at various managerial levels, and to facilitate transfer of knowledge and skills from large foreign and domestic investors to local small and medium enterprises."*

An assessment of local content in  completed in March, 2013 identifies a number of issues including the need to clarify key terms in it as well as noting the need for a system of monitoring and outreach.

It is planned to undertake the revision of the policy, identification of the institutional needs of the MTI and other MDAs in order to undertake development, outreach and monitoring of local content. The design of a communications strategy for outreach to communities, companies and small businesses in order to promote an understanding of local content opportunities will be most useful. Legislative and regulatory issues across various MDAS will also help make the case. Right now, every group seems to have their own interpretation of what Local Content should entail. This confusion should stop.

The Local content policy must be applauded and made to work. The Government through the MTI should however put measures in place to ensure it is well implemented and avoid "Reform capture" by various players for personal gain whilst at the same time putting the hands of investors to the fire to follow through on the tenets of the policy.

## ASP LENGOR'S COMMENDABLE ROAD GAME

A Policeman as inventor?-probably an oxymoron. I was very impressed with ASP Lengor's new invention of a road game which he touted over Radio Democracy. This is a game like "Snakes and Ladders" that teaches people about the driving code to ostensibly make it easier to pass the driving test. You start off with an initial fund of 400 bucks or so which you expend as you go along the route. As you traverse checkpoints, junctions, roundabouts and overtake, you are forced to answer relevant questions on traffic safety, state of the vehicle etc and penalties are dished out. You could go for a replenishment fund to the Bank but really bad violators are kicked out.

It has already been launched and according to Mr. Lengor, the Director General of SLRTA Dr Sarah Bendu and her team are enthused about it. One game has already been given to the Chief Driver- no prizes for guessing!-His Excellency Dr. Ernest Bai

185

Koroma. The game which retails for Le60, 000 is being sold initially in Sierra Leone but may find its way later to other West African countries. I thought Mr. Lengor did a good job of marketing the game.

The texts sent to the studio, the questions by the compares Asma and Storm and ASP Lengor's answers were indeed very enlightening. Most drivers don't know from what lane to overtake, what to do when you get to a roundabout etc. On being asked about traffic lights ASP Lengor said "we are bound to get these one day". A texter opined that licences are bought in any case by paying bribes and there was no need to learn the traffic code. Another asked what should be done about illiterate drivers. Even ASP Lengor found it difficult to answer the question on whether this would be useful for Okada riders or for road users who were constantly "terrorized" by them. In my view Okada riders would completely deplete the Fund and stop the game altogether!

Talking about traffic lights, they seem to be a thing of the past but they were actually working in Freetown. I recall a driver we had at Rutile who came to Freetown, probably for the first time and went back to the mine. "How was Freetown", I asked." Oh, the streets are decorated with lights which keep changing from red to green to other colours-very beautiful!" he replied. "What did you do when you got to them?" I asked." Oh, I just admired them and drove through without stopping", he replied. I was not surprised as he had earlier told me when he saw the dilapidated two storey Bond Street Hotel at Masiaka that he thought he had got to Freetown because he saw an "upgaret". Thankfully, that was his last trip to Freetown.

One burning question I had was whether there were any policemen in the game. Probably some allowance should have been made for leaving unscheduled money at such stops!

Seriously speaking, though, I think ASP Lengor should be commended for his innovation. One very much hopes this game will become more pervasive and that users will put what they have learnt into practice.

Ponder my thoughts.

# October 28, 2013

## VIOLENCE: BREAK DOWN THOSE WALLS

I was invited by the Sierra Leone Network on Small Arms and Light Weapons (SLANSA) two Sundays ago to preach at their thanksgiving service on the theme - "Preventing and reducing violence in the home and community". I chose as a subtheme "Break down those walls" and referenced as scriptural text Ephesians 2 v 14- "Christ himself is our peace. He has destroyed the hate which was like a wall between Jews and Gentiles. So he has made us united."

In the Temple, where the Jews worshipped God, there were different courts (sections). These were:
a)      The Court of the Gentiles;
b)      The Court of the Women;
c)      The Court of the Israelites;
d)      The Court of the Priests;
E)       the Most Holy Place.

Between the Court of the Gentiles and the rest of the Temple there was a wall. The Jews did not allow the Gentiles to pass this wall. There were warning signs on the wall which read: "No man of another race is to proceed within the partition and enclosing wall about the sanctuary. Any one arrested there will have himself to blame for the penalty of death which will be imposed as a consequence." Paul metaphorically says in Ephesians that the coming of Christ broke down that wall between Jews and Gentiles.

No, I am not going to preach another sermon, but I will come back to this passage. Let me however digress and come to the Fourah Bay Community-a community that once prided itself in bringing up disciplined children. A few weeks ago two people were stabbed to death at a football match in Fourah Bay. Some reports say that the machetes used to perpetrate the violence were carried into the field in an icebox by a lady aptly called "dog sh-t". The lawlessness and violence in our communities is getting much too commonplace.

Sierra Leone has been changed by the war, the decline of family life, and the exposure of our young people to different lifestyles. All over the country it is easy to notice that hundreds of thousands of young people basically have nothing to do. Meeting places for young people have now become places of violence.

Sexual abuse is even more common now. Every day we hear about rape stories. Domestic violence, which includes physical, emotional or verbal, economic and sexual abuse is on the rise. Domestic violence complaints in the country increased from 2% in 2010 to 4.7% in 2011 and 6.8% in 2012. Six years after the enactment of the Domestic Violence Act of 2007, gender-based violence (GBV), especially against women, remains a serious concern. In 2007, the Family Support Unit (FSU) became an independent unit of the Sierra Leone Police. The enactment of the new Gender Act and Child Rights Act further broadened the mandate of the FSU. The vision of the FSU, to create a violence-free society by eradicating or minimizing the incidences of sexual and domestic violence, child abuse and child offences in Sierra Leone is still a forlorn one. Of the 4,000 cases of suspected domestic violence investigated by the Police in 2012, only 800 people were charged. Last week, one advocacy group on sexual violence in Moyamba lamented the fact that there had been no High Court sitting in the District for the past nine months.

A whole host of reasons may be responsible for community violence. These include the parlous state of the educational system, unemployment, the economic situation and lack of community cohesion which lead to problems of indiscipline and immorality, several groups should have a role to play to address this issue-religious and community organisations and government. These groups may not be talking to each other on some of these problems, and youths who are the main perpetrator are often left on their own.

There is poor dialogue and interaction with youths in various communities. Also evident is the breakdown of family life in many communities and poor dialogue between spouses. In real life we often have a great propensity to create boundaries. It helps us to feel we are in control. We can fashion reality after our own desires, illusions and fears. There are gender lines, age lines, religious lines, class lines. It is so hard to let go of our lines. There are walls in homes. There is hostility and hatred and defiance and suspicion and distrust between husbands and wives, between parents and children, and between us as neighbours.

Many people know someone who is experiencing domestic violence but choose not to talk. We need to assure them they do not deserve such abuse. In many communities today we build walls. Instead of protecting ourselves from some cherished values, we may instead find out that we have ended up tearing down things of value from within ourselves. Martin Luther King talked about "making our neighbourhood into a brotherhood."

That is why I have been very impressed by the Press Release from the "Fourah Bay Community Foundation", part of which reads:

"The Imams, the Alkadi, the elders, the Jammats of the Fourah Bay Community and the Fourah Bay Community Foundation condemn in the strongest possible terms the spate of indiscipline, the lawlessness and the violence that is perpetrated in and around the community over the past several months which has resulted in malicious wounding and death. The people of Fourah Bay are peace loving and law abiding. We pride ourselves with integrity and high moral standards. We would not want our community to degenerate into lawlessness and anarchy."

Here are some of their resolutions in the Press Release:
"1. That each house in the Fourah Bay community as demarcated be issued with a warning letter informing the households that any evil-doer, gangster or anyone found wanting or suspected of involvement in gang warfare must be reported to the police, otherwise the house owner or caretaker shall be held responsible.
2. That the Fourah Bay Community Foundation endeavours to outreach youth groups in the community so that exchange of information would be facilitated and enhanced and that the Foundation considers having a youth wing in its structure.
3. That the elders Imams and other stakeholders continue to listen and dialogue with youths in their group."

Organisations like SLANSA, a national coalition of religious institutions and civil organisations and networks to promote and popularise human security through advocacy and micro disarmament for small arms and light weapons (SALW) control are trying to address problems like the easy availability of SALW which escalate conflicts. Community action taken by groups like the one in Fourah Bay should break down those walls in the communities and take a holistic look at the problem of community violence. The Churches and Mosques must also speak out. Paul's message in Ephesians to break down those walls is indeed apt for all of us.

## LET THE DEAD NOT BURY THEIR DEAD

I don't derive pleasure in the macabre but I have heard some morbid stories lately related to exhumation of dead bodies that concern me. The first was on the popular radio programme "Monologue" from its Port Loko correspondent about a "plane crash"-yes plane crash! The story goes that there had been a plane crash of a "witch plane" in which 15 people are reported to have been involved. The ghost of one person who had died in the "crash" and had been buried had been harassing many people in his neighbourhood, especially those with whom he had some gripe when alive. The Chiefs had got in touch with his family to exhume the body. This had been done and the body found not to be decomposed even after two weeks of burial. The solution to this problem, according to some "Ariogbos" contacted was to mutilate the body. I don't know how exactly he said this was resolved but there was greater fear of a particular woman also involved in the crash and who was hospitalised and at the point of death. According to the reporter, she would probably be a bigger bundle of trouble when she died as she had a longer list of enemies.

In the second, a local chief in Lumley was quoted thus: "The chief told the nation that their cemetery is overflowing – the dead are not allowed to rest before their bones are removed for other bodies to be buried."

Let's leave the plane crash to the Police, Civil Aviation Authorities or any Government Department with expertise in sniffing out ghost workers, for want of better evidence, and concentrate on the latter issue-shortage of grave space. The number of grave yards will never be able to hold everybody who dies unless there are multiple burials in one grave or we extensively practise cremation. I believe that in Sierra Leone, desecration or removal of a body could result in being sued. Reuse of graves is common in most of Europe. I am not an expert in taphonomy (the study of what happens to bodies after they are buried). My research however tells me an adult corpse without a coffin buried six feet deep will usually take five to ten years to turn into a skeleton. Even though some 70 % of bodies in places like Britain are cremated, there will obviously be widespread resistance to cremation in this country because of cultural and religious reasons. The reuse of graves is more by happenstance as some relatives may neglect tending to the graves of relatives over time. Whatever the solution, it is high time we started thinking about a solution to this as our population grows.

And by the way, how did that reporter know it was a 15 seater plane?

Ponder my thoughts.

# November 5, 2013

## FOOD SECURITY: NOT ABOUT RICE BUT POVERTY

"I encourage our people to change their eating habit and alternate rice with other crops grown in the country, such as yam, cassava and sweet potato, among others." This recent statement is attributed to the Minister of Agriculture, Forestry and Food Security Dr. Joseph Sam Sesay. Detractors were quick on the draw to remind him about earlier statements attributed to him about the country having almost attained self-sufficiency in rice production. One report says he recently said that rice production has increased by about 30% and that in the not too distant future, Sierra Leone will start exporting rice.

We have seen a lot of frantic activities on the Agriculture front. The government claims the introduction of the Small-Holder Commercialization projects has generally given support to rural farmers and helped them get their crops to the markets. The development of agricultural business centres (ABCs), which are owned and managed by farmer-based organisations to deliver services such as micro-credit, sale of inputs, rental of labour-saving equipment, storage of seeds and food to reduce post-harvest losses and transportation of harvests to markets to smallholder farmers should ostensibly result in greater output and impact the food security situation positively. Coupled with the increase in the Agriculture budget, the mechanisation schemes and other programmes, these are all probably all good initiatives if well implemented.

Sierra Leone annually requires nearly 500 000 tonnes of milled rice, the main staple food, to feed its population and imports a fair percentage of that. The call by Dr Sesay to give consideration to alternating rice with other potential staple foods is not a new one and is in fact in line with the food diversification strategy which is enshrined in our food security strategy.

Many people however complain about the cost of some of these alternative foodstuffs. Though readily available for purchase in places like Moyamba junction, cassava, yams and some of these alternative foodstuffs may be affordable for fairly affluent urban dwellers to buy when travelling from rural areas or from urban markets, but may be beyond the reach of poor people. Many complain they may not be in fact be cheaper than rice. Besides, some of them may be seasonal. The logical question to ask then is "Is there enough food to go around?" The simple answer, according to the most recent World Food programme (WFP) report is "No!"

The WFP report essentially attributes our food insecurity problems to our poverty. Food prices have remained high, with a yearly food inflation of up to 13.3%. Households spend on average 63% of their total expenditure on food. Some 53% of Sierra Leoneans in fact borrow money to buy food. Three quarters of the population rely on markets as their main source of food. Petty traders, farmers and unskilled labourers suffer most from food insecurity with well over 50 % of each of these groups being food insecure.

Some 70% of the population live below the national poverty line of US$2 day- poverty is the most prevalent cause of food insecurity in the country. The Comprehensive Food Security and Vulnerability Analysis survey (CFSVA 2011) found out that nationally almost half (45%) of households or 2.5 million people are classified as food insecure during the lean season, reflecting seasonal food access issues. Of those about 374,000 people (6.5%) are severely food insecure. Hunger peaks in August with people's access to food starting to deteriorate in June and July. Hunger is indeed endemic.

Figures for District vulnerability (2008 figures but may not have not changed markedly) make for an interesting read. The districts most affected by food insecurity are Pujehun (80%), Moyamba (76%), and Tonkolili (74%). The least affected districts are Kailahun (21%), Western Rural (22%), Western Urban (23%) and Bonthe (23%). The Western Slum is 40% food insecure. Rural households are more food insecure than urban (54% versus 29%).

The Sierra Leone Demographic and Health Survey (SLDHS 2008) revealed that 36% of Sierra Leonean children are stunted. Almost one-fifth of them are underweight, with 7% classified as severely underweight. Insufficient access to food at the household level by large parts of the population could be attributed to: (1) lack of financial resources to purchase food on a continuous basis and 2) lack of physical access to the food due to inadequate infrastructure such as markets and roads to transport the food, lack of storage facilities and high post-harvest losses resulting in high food prices.

It is ironical that our very own food producers-the farmers are the most food insecure. The incidence of poverty is highest in the agricultural sector, with about 79% of those engaged in the sector being poor.

Ensuring that the current initiatives are well implemented and problems of infrastructure, storage facilities to prevent farmers from selling their surpluses in the immediate post-harvest season, provision of agriculture inputs and the other initiatives will obviously be of immense help. Our food insecurity problems should however not be laid at the doorstep of the Agriculture Ministry alone. It needs a holistic approach also to get most of our compatriots out of poverty. Food security is not just about rice substitution; rather it is about the efficacy of the production and marketing process and above all getting us over the poverty line.

## TONTAK ALI   10 SIERRA QUEENS 0

Yes, I know you will say it is against their Nigerian counterparts that our female U20 national team lost so woefully, but be a little patient with our girls, as there may have been more opponents than Nigerian girls.

I am no stranger to being walloped in the sporting arena. I recall our sports Master at CKC, who after two failed attempts to play against the Bo School in Bo because of the riotous conduct of some students, was preparing the team to play in a neutral ground at Njala University. One sure way of breaking (yes, as in BREAK) "Possible Deen's" legs was to recruit the largest boy in the school into the football team. "Lewis can charge", he confidently bragged before the match. The rest is history and I will not reveal the score. One thing I learnt though-Lewis did not get within a yard of "Possible Deen" for the whole of the first half, he was on field. He however succeeded in creating a few craters with his boot from charging imaginary opponents. The object lesson for me was that you had to train well and have the necessary skills in any sport.

True to form, the SLFA has fired its main culprit, the coach, Hannah Williams for "failing to provide technical leadership". Just when I thought I had assimilated their rationale, there came another Press release which said "Coach Williams administered certain medication to the entire squad which rendered them ineffective to match their Nigerian counterparts. The drug TONKAT ALI is primarily used to increase the flow of blood to and from the heart and also to excite her sexually. The purpose of administering the drug to the players was to enhance their performance, from technical reports submitted....the girls appeared unfocused, unusual and jaded as a result of unusual menstruation and diarrhoea due to the side effect of the drug." No comments on this as my head still spins!

Some of my cyber friends have been sympathetic. One made light of the situation: "But again, these are Sierra Leonean girls we are talking about. They are strong and are probably laughing and "provoking" each other.....We don't get depressed.....that's for the sissy kids of the West. ........It's just a game, these kids would say. Una lef dem. Den done forget sef. Salone pikin ba... ". Another feels so sorry for them "As a parent of a former girl soccer player, I am heartbroken for these girls. It is unconscionable to deny our youth preparation and send them into international competition to fly the flag. It hurts them and the flag. In countries that are serious about their image and their youth, heads would roll for such irresponsible cruel act."

Whatever one's position, the Sierra Queens can take heart from some famous international defeats. In 2001, the Australian and American Samoa national association football teams played in a qualifying match for the 2002 FIFA World Cup. Australia set a world record for the largest victory in an international football match, winning the game 31–0. In the 1974 World Cup Yugoslavia beat Zaire 9-0.

Someone writing on the net on the same issue says Nigeria's women lost 7-1 to USA in the 1999 world cup, 5-0 in 2003, 1-0 in 2007 and in 2010 went on to beat USA. Take heart, girls!

Unlike boys, girls don't grow up playing soccer so they have to learn the game and then develop their reflexes. Boys already have the reflexes developed by the time they are 7. Whatever the case it is obvious these girls needed better training to play against Nigeria, one of the best female teams in the world. They should have probably been given enough time to prepare. I hope this defeat will not dent the confidence of our girls. Again, one notable football cognoscenti opined "A domestic league from U 17 to senior female football would have helped; a selection of players camped and trained for a period and the best chosen for further opportunities say in Nigeria, Ghana and South Africa...another option. Investment in their education might have been a major priority at this time...and then plan a two year introduction into international football..." he is probably right.

Whatever the case, SLFA seems satisfied with ousting its *bete noir*, Hannah Williams and putting her TONKA ALI concoction in the bin. Time however to think this problem through some more!

Ponder my thoughts

# November 12, 2013

## MCC SCORES: RAMIFICATION FOR SIERRA LEONE

I am still hoping that my country will qualify for the MCC compact award which will undoubtedly bode well for us. One can be excused for being unfazed with the temporary setback that will make the hill considerably steeper to climb for us to achieve our objectives, albeit with the caveat that government puts the bad parts of the results in the "important lessons learnt for action" category.

I am however not so much interested in the mechanism of getting there, as this can be explained better by others more versed in the niceties of how a country eventually qualifies. I would rather be preoccupied with what the scores say about how our country is governed. One has long since lost faith in most of our internal monitoring and evaluation mechanisms especially those bordering on government performance.

The MCC indicators do in fact inform us about how well our broad policy framework encourages poverty reduction through economic growth. This can also be a tool for us in our varied spheres of life and our government to monitor performance and advocate for continued policy reform. The indicators are independently and transparently developed by third-parties that measure our demonstrated commitment to just and democratic governance, investments in our people, and economic freedom.

To judge performance on the policy indicators, a country should perform above the median or absolute threshold on at least half of the indicators, above the median on the Control of Corruption indicator, and above the absolute threshold on either the Civil Liberties or Political Rights indicators.

The following indicators are measured by MCC in the three categories of Ruling Justly, Investing in People, and Encouraging Economic Freedom.

**Ruling Justly**-These indicators measure just and democratic governance, including a country's demonstrated commitment to promoting political pluralism, equality, and the rule of law; respecting human and civil rights; protecting private property rights; encouraging transparency and accountability of government; and combating corruption.

**Civil Liberties**—Countries are rated on: freedom of expression; association and organizational rights; rule of law and human rights; and personal autonomy and economic rights, among other things.

**Political Rights**—Independent experts rate countries on: the prevalence of free and fair elections of officials with real power; the ability of citizens to form political parties that may compete fairly in elections; freedom from domination by the military, foreign powers, totalitarian parties, and the political rights of minority groups, among other things.

So how did we fare? First the good news. We passed on inflation, regulatory quality, trade policy, girl's education completion rate, gender in the economy, political rights, civil liberties, freedom of information, and access to credit, business start up and the rule of law. The government has been able to keep inflation below 15%. Our investment in the education of the girl child seems to be yielding dividends. Several initiatives in doing business, making us rise in rankings have borne fruit. We still have a relatively free press and despite our upheavals the rule of law can be said to prevail in this country.

The not so good news! We have failed on nine of these scores in the following areas: fiscal policy, health expenditure, primary education, natural resources protection, immunisation rates, child health, land rights and access, government effectiveness and control of corruption.

Cutting out the needless jargon and putting things simply, it is telling us the following:

**Fiscal Policy** - Government borrowing is high. We are probably trying to live beyond our means and may be too ambitious with the projects we have undertaken.

**Health expenditure**-The total expenditure on health is low and we are not providing quality health care. Also child mortality rates are high. This is not surprising- the parlous state of our health facilities and poor commitment by health provision personnel remain serious concerns. Sierra Leone's health expenditure levels are still considerable short of the 15 % of the national budget required as per the Abuja declaration.

**Primary education**-The promotion of broad-based primary education remains poor and total expenditure on primary education is low. This is not that surprising as education seems to have been put on the back burner.

**Natural resources protection** -This refers mainly to the sustainable management of natural resources which mainly pertains to the protection of our tropical rainforests. The high rate of deforestation and difficulty in meeting the requirements of various related international conventions to which we are signatory will make it difficult to achieve this.

**Immunization Rates** – We need to achieve a 90 percent immunisation rate, which we have not done.

**Child Health** - This index is made up of three indicators - access to improved water, access to improved sanitation, and child (ages 1-4) mortality. There are improvements being pursued but we are still a long way off the mark.

**Land Rights and Access**— This rates countries on the extent to which the institutional, legal, and market frameworks provide secure land tenure and equitable access to land in rural areas, and the time and cost of property registration in urban and peri-urban areas. Land problems currently abound in all spheres and are being constantly aired in the media. How the new land policy will address these problems is anyone's guess.

**Government Effectiveness**—This is an index of surveys and expert assessments that rate countries on: the quality of public service provision; civil servants' competency and independence from political pressures; and the government's ability to plan and implement sound policies, among other things. Our failure in this area indicates that we need to jerk ourselves from our slumber and have the political will to address many of our thorny problems.

**Control of Corruption**— Countries are rated on: "grand corruption" in the political arena; the frequency of petty corruption; the effects of corruption on the business environment; and the tendency of elites to engage in "state capture," among other things. It is a very important consideration for qualifying for the MCC. Failing this does not say much for our fight against corruption.

How do we compare to other nations in the sub-region? Liberia has also failed on a considerable number of the indices-11 out of the 20. They have however passed on the all important corruption index. It is also noteworthy that they have passed on health expenditure. Of course as would be expected, Ghana, which had received its compact award long ago has dusted its heels and left us behind passing on all except fiscal policy, primary school expenditure and trade policy.

Time for action by Government!

## POLITICIANS AND MONEY: FROM GHANA WITH LOVE

Robert James Manion, in "Gentlemen, Players and Politicians quipped:" "No man should enter politics unless he is independently rich or independently poor." The case of Ms. Victoria Hammah, an erstwhile Deputy Minister in Ghana has recently brought the issue of politicians and money to the fore. Ms. Hannah was fired just one day after the tape which contains her $1m-making ambition went viral on social media. It was also played on a local radio station. On the tape, which is suspected to have been made by her driver, she is quoted as saying, "If you have money then you can control people."

Apparently, Ms. Hammah is no stranger to controversy. She apparently said last August there was pressure on her to steal public money because people believed that, being a Minister, she was rich. Not everyone seems to be knocking Ms. Hammah, however. Kwame Mayo, the Ghanaian-born "AMERICA'S MANDELA" opined thus: "It should be noted that Ms Victoria Hammah could have used Politics to make $ 1 Million through writing Best Seller Books !!!", in his new Book captioned : "Politics $1 Million Dollars --- The Untold Story of a Gorgeous Woman, Who Drowned in Africa's Men Only --- High Seas of Corruption". "Unless there is Evidence to prove that Ms. Victoria Hammah was engaged in Corruption, Civility of Democracy demands that she should not have been fired for merely Day-Dreaming to become a Millionaire, or engaging in a private conversation".

Poor Ms. Hammah, a rising star in President Mahama's government after having campaigned so hard for him is now sidelined for "dreaming out loud" about money. To say that politicians like money is an understatement. One source quotes: "In many advanced countries, people with money enter politics but there are many instances in which people enter politics in both advanced and developing countries (especially in the latter) to make money. Many Americans grumble about the wealth of their politicians, but they are paupers compared with their Chinese counterparts. The 50 richest members of America's Congress are worth $1.6 billion in all. In China, the wealthiest 50 delegates to the National People's Congress, the rubber-stamp parliament, control $94.7 billion."

In many countries including ours that could ill afford it, we see "independently poor politicians becoming "dependently" rich". It is however difficult to catch them with their fingers in the till. Many engage in different kinds of corruption including bribery, extortion, cronyism, patronage and sometimes outright embezzlement. In Ghana the Member of Parliament for Berekum East, Dr. Kwabena Twum Nuamah is quoted as saying that society is to be blamed for the massive corruption in his country-"In Ghana now, it pays to be corrupt because the society itself is pushing to be corrupt. If you are in government and you are not corrupt, you become the odd one out and so everyone is trying very hard to be corrupt", he stated. "We live in a country, where when you are given a position in government, people think it is an opportunity for you to amass wealth. Our mindset is pushing politicians to become corrupt", he bemoaned.

Whatever the truth of the matter, the fact remains that Ms. Hammah has lost her job. Wondering aloud what would have happened, had this been a Sierra Leonean politician, a political friend quipped: "BOKU TALK, BOKU TALK. If you yams white, cobar am!" How one wishes he had advised poor Ms. Hammah!

Ponder my thoughts

# November 19, 2013


## BAI BUREH COMPLAINS TO CHURCHILL

Bai Bureh was a warrior
He fought against the British
"The British gee am one slap
Eahalakortormaimu"

This familiar derogatory refrain was used to exemplify how we have denigrated our historical icons, by the renowned African studies Scholar and historian C.Magbale Fyle in a speech he gave on the relevance of our history and culture to our development. He was particularly miffed with the ABC Secretariat which he said was going in the wrong direction in trying to convince Sierra Leoneans to change their attitude and behaviour. The ABC secretariat, according to him was not properly equipped. In his view the attitudes and behaviour of our people determine how well they will function in whatever endeavour they find themselves. "This needs to be elaborately taught to our people, to the children in the school system, so that they grow up believing in these values. Nationalism will create a sense of civic responsibility. Symbols we create, national figures we idolize, have to be presented in a national context", according to Professor Fyfe. He concludes: "There is a strong need for a re-valorisation of our cultural and historical traditions......our symbols, national figures should be presented in a national context"

Bai Bureh organised resistance against the British in 1898 as he and others stood up to the British who required them to pay taxes to them for their own houses. Although Bai Bureh put up a brave fight, superior weapons used by the British and the scorched earth policy they adopted finally led to his capitulation after ten months. At the heart of the matter though is that people like Bai Bureh, Nyagua of Panguma and Kpana Lewis stood up to the British for what was essentially the British foisting their will on our people and impugning our national sovereignty. The fact that people like these have not received the recognition due them speaks volumes for the way we have mishandled our history and allowed it to be taught through someone else's lens. Even our educated elite help perpetuate such a psyche.

Prof. Fyfe is right. In fact we have given little attention to civic education. Essentially civic education is concerned with three different elements: civic knowledge, civic skills and civic disposition. Civic knowledge refers to citizens' understanding of the workings of the political system and of their own political and civic rights and responsibilities. Civic skills refer to the ability of citizens to analyze, evaluate, take and defend positions on public issues, and to use their knowledge to participate in civic and political matters. Civic dispositions are defined as the citizen traits necessary for a democracy (e.g. tolerance, public spiritedness, civility, critical mindedness and willingness to listen, negotiate, and compromise).

Unfortunately the civic education taught in schools has been severely watered down. It is now part of the social studies curriculum. Very little emphasis is placed especially on civic dispositions and issues that would make us nationalistic and eschew some of the ills that are permeating our society are often skated over. Nationalism simply means showing unconditional love for your country, and putting your country first or above personal interest. It means making sacrifices for your country, and being prepared and willing to defend your country at anytime and at all costs. A suitable curriculum should cover issues such as civility, courage, self-discipline, concern for the common good, respect for other and other traits relevant to citizenship.

A positive passion for the public good, the public interest established in the minds of people and focusing on character and civic virtue will make one view things in a national perspective in future life. Questions the citizen may ask himself/herself may include:

a) In accepting such a huge bribe, are thousands of my country folk going to suffer immeasurably because teachers will not get paid? b) In cutting down electricity pylons to make pots or stealing oil from transformers am I going to deprive several people of electricity supply c) If I give out jobs only to people of my own ethnic group or political party, what do I expect to happen if another party were to come to power?

We should obviously make a conscious national effort to revalorize our history and traditions. The question then arises: Who and what do we revalorize? This decision is not easy in the light of our various national schisms, a dearth of who we may consider heroes or role models and our poor performance in various spheres. Thinking about it carefully we should perhaps also consider figures associated with ending the ten year rebel war. There are those worthy of adulation for their gallantry in pursuing the war or who played a direct role in bringing the peace. This may however evoke arguments from several quarters as we may have realized, that may not be easy to resolve. Our history is also replete with sports figures initially adulated and then disparaged.

We have the occasional flashes of brilliance that would put us on a pedestal on a regional or world scale. Prof. Monty Jones' role with the Nerica rice or the brilliant inventor, Kelvin Doe come to mind. On the other hand there are our national historical assets which could do us proud and remind us of where we came from. Unfortunately, many historical monuments lie in ruins and are in no way linked to our teaching of our history to our young folks or to a potentially lucrative tourist industry.

How many of us actually do sing the national anthem in a non perfunctory way, thinking about the meaning of the words? Why have the fine words in our national pledge almost been abandoned?

I pledge my love and loyalty to my country Sierra Leone;
I vow to serve her faithfully at all times;
I promise to defend her honour and good name Always work for her unity peace, freedom and prosperity And put her interest above all else.
So help me God.

Our sporting prowess which once saw us rally round our national football team with nationalistic fervour has now been reduced to a parody. In short there are very few issues which make us rally round "singing thy praise O native land".

The government may want to give consideration to a knowledgeable panel of experts to think through these issues and make recommendations on how we can instil a sense of nationalism in our citizenry and broadly agree on which national symbols to tout as well as national heroes to idolise. These must be presented in a national context. This will not be easy as they may probably be engaged in needless rancour especially on those to idolise. They should however be reminded of the words of one historian who concluded: "Great men are not often good men". There is a tinge of truism in this. Both Abraham Lincoln and Winston Churchill who loom large over the history of the USA and Britain respectively for their immense contributions to the survival of their countries were flawed characters in many areas of their lives.

Lincoln's Gettysburg address is etched in the consciousness of American children- "Fourscore and seven years ago our fathers brought forth on this continent, a new nation, conceived in Liberty, and dedicated to the proposition that all men are created equal........ ." William Buckley speaking in Boston in 1995 to the Churchill society illustrates the flawed character issue well in his talk titled "Let us now praise famous men". He said: "It is my proposal that Churchill's words were indispensable to the benediction of that hour which we hail here tonight as we hail the memory of the man who spoke them, as we come together to praise him."

If we think hard about how people like Bai Bureh were "indispensable to the benediction of the hour" perhaps we should not be singing:

"The British gee am one slap
Eahalakortormaimu"

## MY HERO SALIMATU

We must often wonder who we have idolised over the ages. We have the familiar figures in our history and civic books. Bai Bureh, Madam Yoko, Sir Milton Margai etc. -these are more historical figures who helped make out history what it is. In contemporary life, people are more likely to idolise sporting or musical figures and want to be like them. One thing that has always intrigued me is how we decide on which sporting heroes to idolise. I've often wondered why Sierra Leone football players like using false names. Quite often it could be a foreign name after some notable player like Garrincha, Pele, and Tastao etc. Some may say it is quite understandable if they have no local player of yore they would like to emulate.

It however gets even more confusing when they use a local name perhaps descriptive of some attitude they have. It is however hard to understand how they came about names like Tumbu, Tamba goat, Gbanaloko etc. Unfortunately (perhaps fortunately) they don't use these names on their vests and foreign commentators use their actual names-just as well-I would hate to see "T-goat" at the back of a vest. It gets confusing when you are more used to a local playing name only to have the player referred to as a Kamara or Conteh.

Anyway I can't say I blame them. It took me some time during my younger days to find out the team my friends and I idolised was not "Hassana" but "Arsenal". And then the most confusing one when we were playing "bite game" and referring to ourselves by names of notable foreign players was the realisation that my hero was not in fact SALIMATU as most of my fellow players would call themselves but STANLEY MATTHEWS, the legendary English winger. Never mind there was a time I liked being SALIMATU.

Ponder my thoughts

# November 26, 2013

## CKC@60. DIAMONDJUBILEE

Sixty years ago, a Catholic Institution was founded in Bo. The intention of the founding fathers, the Catholic Church was to create a veritable centre of learning that will produce students who will contribute meaningfully to the development of Sierra Leone and the spiritual growth of the Catholic Church. Sixty years hence the school continues to achieve its objectives, though it has been caught up in the social and economic vicissitudes in which our country has been mired.

Old students trooped to Bo last week to celebrate the diamond jubilee of this great school. CKC is a school that has produced students who are actively participating in all spheres of life in Sierra Leone. Five out of the seven heads of the science departments at FBC are CKC alumni. The school can boast of top class engineers, doctors, lawyers and people in other professions servings at home and abroad.

The speech day and prize giving ceremony was chaired by an illustrious old boy, Professor Gbamanja, with Dr Kandeh Yumkella as the guest speaker. Former Vice President Solomon Berewa, a Foundation Student of the school and its first graduate, who spoke at the fundraising dinner was enthused about what CKC had done for him. The rigorous education and discipline that was meted out to him by the Catholic priests who manned the school had prepared him well for later life. That he had risen to the second highest position in the land was due in no small measure to CKC. Dr Yumkella spoke of the role CKC had played in shaping his life- "I firmly believe that one must have a strong sense of responsibility and a commitment to a set of core values in order to achieve success. CKC taught me to have a sense of responsibility at a very early age", he said.

The week-long celebrations culminated in a Church service and March past- which was more or less a carnival through the streets of Bo.

Celebrations apart, the reality is that a school which once prided itself as the premier science institution in the provinces now has a decrepit laboratory and an infrastructure that is bursting at the seams. The two shift system has not only resulted in students going to class at odd hours, but also resulted in lower contact hours. A significant proportion of the teachers still remain unpaid at the end of the month as they have not been "verified". This is a familiar litany in nearly all schools now. It is not therefore surprising that the thrust of the old boys' efforts has been on trying to maintain standards in the light of a national decline in educational standards. CKC has a vibrant alumni association, COBA with large overseas branches in the US and UK. The vibrant President, John Bosco Kaikai has overseen projects related to improving the school infrastructure and providing educational and other materials for the school.

The old students have rallied round and contributed generously. The project for building extra classrooms and fencing the compound was launched at the anniversary dinner. The Alumni association always rises up to the challenges of the day. When I was president of the association in the early 90s the challenge was late payment of teachers' salaries which prompted us to set up a revolving salary scheme. We have had an illustrious group of presidents from Solomon Berewa to Charles Margai to John Aruna, J.B. Vandy Dauda, Sam Stevens, Sam Macarthy, and Dr Kakpindi Soyei, to name few.

The vibrancy of our overseas branches is second to none, and perhaps what is even more surprising is the ardent role played by Old girls (even though the Association in a sexist way is still an "Old boys Association"). The UK Branch was ably represented by Kankay Hubbard, whilst old girls like Sia Matturi Josiah continue to play a leading role in the US Branch. There are old students in these Braches who will give an arm and a leg for CKC-people like Anthony Sheriff come to mind.

A surprising fact about CKC though is the active participation of its alumni in politics. I do not wish to needlessly pursue this angle, as an alumni Association should really be about the camaraderie amongst its membership and their joint commitment to the furtherance of the ideals of the school. I agree entirely with my friend and fellow alumnus Charlie Hughes when he warned in an article "This college has outstanding representatives at the helm of every scientific field around the world today..........In our obsession with politics we totally forget about the global citizens that the school has produced for this country. I do not by any means desire to denigrate political achievement. But it is only acceptable if we put education first. And it is well and good if educational achievement props a politician's political achievement." I must however beg Charlie to veer a little towards the political as it did portend to dominate the celebrations-thankfully it didn't.

Sometimes as has been seen from the Solomon Berewa vs Charles Margai saga, "brother has been pitched against brother". If rumours are to be believed, there may be as many as four alumni in the next SLPP Presidential aspirant race-one more than the last time! (I am still in the process of trying to confirm their names). But what makes a school, more renowned for its prowess in the sciences produce an inordinately large number of old students who have a bent for politics. Perhaps a quote from Dr. Yumkella's speech attempts to answer this question: "With a strong sense of Responsibility, a sense of Proportion, commitment to Partnerships, a readiness to serve others, commitment to Hard Work, a solid Education, and unwavering Faith in the Power of the Almighty are the keys to success and prosperity for you and me." Perhaps it is this "readiness to serve others... and unwavering faith in the power of the almighty" that is spurring them on. Belief in divine power is central to the CKC ethos as exemplified in a quote from Robert Boyle in the hallway leading to the lab: "I should be much better content to see you ignore the mystery of nature than deny the author of it".

The interest in politics is not only restricted to national politics but also to local politics. Both Mayor Harold tucker of Bo and District Council Chairman of Kailahun, Alex Bhonapha are CKC alumni. The Chief Administrator of the Bo City Council and most of his staff are CKC alumni. The foundation group of the PMDC had a group of mainly "young turks" who were CKC alumni. Most of them still continue to play active roles in the national political landscape-Former Ministers Dr Soccoh Kabia, Steve Ngaujia, John Saad and current Minister Arrow Bockarie as well as the equally political Aggrey Aruna, who at that time believed in Charles Margai's "message" are members of this group. Incidentally, Charles Margai was "Missing in Action".

The oft asked question before the celebrations was whether Dr Yumkella was going to make some declaration of sorts. They need not have worried. His speech was measured and apt for the occasion-CKC boys are probably too smart to call a spade a spade. Whatever else one may want to read from his speech could best be explained by the biblical maxim "He that has ears to hear, let him hear". We did have time to hobnob with each other during the reunion night and it was good to see most of these political figures I have mentioned, Kandeh Yumkella and fellow alumni reminisce and wax nostalgic about their time at school without so much as a whiff of politics. Kandeh reminded me about how he used to sweep under my bed (he was in the second form when I was in sixth form). I retorted that he may never be willing to sweep under my bed again-nar big man now!

CKC has also been gradually achieving its objective of contributing to the spiritual growth of the Catholic Church. About 36 of the Catholic Priests produced since the indigenisation of the Church are CKC alumni. I rather like Dr Sylvester Yankuba's appreciation of what the Catholic Church did for CKC in a recent speech in London-"Foremost, it goes without saying that, any accrued CKC legacies are ultimately owed to the Catholic missionary *"Congregatio Sancti Spiritus"* Priests (or "Holy Ghost Fathers") – mostly from Ireland – who, all those years ago, went over to Sierra Leone and there endeavoured to help make the lot of Sierra Leoneans a better one by setting up schools such as CKC. Clearly, therefore, I am sure you will all agree that those priests truly deserve both our unqualified gratitude and our most hearty plaudits!"

I also rather like Dr. Yankuba's advice to fellow alumni: "To end then, I will contend that, as well as preserving our ethos, values and achievements, only by also preserving the physical fabric as well as the infrastructure of CKC continually, can we vouchsafe the preservation of its tripartite heritage of Enlightenment, Philanthropy and Leadership."

Let us continue to preserve our enlightenment, philantrophy and leadership as old Boys and Girls of the school-values that were taught us by Father Corbett, Father Lambe, Father Curran, Gabriel Amara and all those Principals and teachers who helped shape us for the future.

Adveniat regnum tuum.

Ponder my thoughts.

# December 3, 2013

## ELECTION PETITION VERDICT: "THE LAW IS AN ASS"

Charles Dickens was probably not way off the mark when he used the phrase, "the law is an ass" in his 1838 novel, Oliver Twist. Whether we like it or not, we are a country of laws, hence we abide by what we may consider absurd court rulings, and appeal, if we consider it advisable. The expression refers to the application of the law that is contrary to common sense. In Oliver Twist, Mr. Bumble, the unhappy spouse of a domineering wife, is told in court that "...the law supposes that your wife acts under your direction". "If the law supposes that," said Mr. Bumble, squeezing his hat emphatically in both hands, "the law is an ass—an idiot. If that's the eye of the law, the law is a bachelor; and the worst I wish the law is that his eye may be opened by experience—by experience."

To many people the recent ruling in the election petition cases involving constituencies 05 and 15 defy logic. To put things in the layman's language, two SLPP MPs who were not awarded party symbols to contest the last general elections took the designated party candidates in their respective constituencies and NEC to court with the objective of restraining them from contesting the elections, as according to them they had flouted party and/or national election laws and regulations. The judge ordered an injunction for these candidates not to contest the elections. NEC found it difficult to fully comply, as according to them, ballot papers bearing the candidates' names had already been printed. Despite attempts made to cross their names out on the ballot paper and last minute radio advisory broadcasts, these proved not to be effective and people voted overwhelmingly for these candidates. According to constituency based reports, the SLPP candidate in Constituency 5 scored some 11,000 votes against the APC's 2,400. In Constituency 15, the SLPP candidate scored some 9,000 to the APC's 4000.

The court ruling finally came some fifteen months after the elections. Though concluding that the cases against the defendants had no merit, the learned Judge, Justice Showers ordered that the SLPP candidates' votes be nullified and the results of the elections read. This in effect meant that the APC candidates who were a distant second (had the votes been valid) had won the elections with less that 20% of the votes in one constituency and 35% in the other of the total votes cast. The SLPP and several independent observers have been stupefied by this judgment which essentially gives the APC two more seats in Parliament on a legal "technicality".

Let us examine the courses of action closer. If there was time for NEC to carry out the court's instructions to the full and there was no evidence of the SLPP candidate on the ballot, people would have gone in to vote for the other candidates. It is not inconceivable that voter turnout would have been less than 30 percent and a winner declared. The court case would have ended with the same results as stated by the court. If the petitioners' cases had no merit, what would have happened if the same result had been declared? Would the results have been nullified and a rerun ordered? One sceptic who is no admirer of our justice system has observed that the same result would have been achieved.

Hailing from constituency 05 in Kailahun, I can affirm from repeated calls from constituents that they do not understand the rationale behind a ruling that essentially disenfranchises them and sends to Parliament as a representative who belongs to a party they overwhelmingly voted against and who got less than 20 percent of their votes. But then, this is the law and as Mr Bumble said, probably not meant to be understood.

There are a few issues of concern with such a ruling. Parliament is a representative institution, which reflects the dictum – "government of the people, by the people for the people". The Member, as an elected representative of his constituents, is an agent for the realisation of the aspirations of his people and the nation at large. In this regard, a Member is enjoined to advocate in Parliament concerns of his constituents. Elections enable voters to select leaders and to hold them accountable for their performance in office. Whatever other needs voters may have, participation in an election serves to reinforce their self-esteem and self-respect. This ruling turns this ideal on its head for both constituencies.

It is also worth mentioning that one of the causes of our recent civil war was the injustice perpetrated, especially at various levels of our governance system. The TRC report states thus: "The judiciary was subordinated to the executive, parliament did little more than 'rubber-stamp', and the civil service became a redundant state machine ........non-state bodies that ought to ensure accountability – like media houses or civil society groups – were thoroughly co-opted...... Lack of courage on the part of lawyers and judges over the years paved the way for the desecration of the constitution, the perpetuation of injustice and the pillaging of the country's wealth." Quite an indictment!

I do not intend to dwell on the legal "correctness" of such a ruling. I can only point to the advice given in the conclusion of the TRC report: "Access to justice can also be achieved through a simplification of legal rules so that they may be understood and used by anyone." Despite the fact that we have a constitution that essentially guarantees representation of the people and we have revamped our electoral laws, to avoid such situations, we have taken a good fifteen months pursuing an electoral case resulting in non representation of constituents in two constituencies. The situation has been further compounded by the order resulting in these constituencies being represented by people for whom less than 20 percent and 35 percent cast their votes. Furthermore we have several normally vociferous groups on other issues who have kept silent on such an important governance issue. One may ask; where is the Body of Christ? where is the Bar association? Where is civil society? Where is the National Commission for Democracy? I never knew I would say this, but thank you Mohamed Bangura. Kudos also to SLPP that despite our internecine warfare, we seem to be united on fighting this menace. But should the SLPP be left alone to fight this noble cause?

The APC has been claiming that the SLPP inflicted this debacle on themselves. "After all the petitioners were ex SLPP MPs", they claim. This may be true. Their case however rings hollow when you consider the following facts 1) the petitioner Ex MP for Constituency 5, Sam May Macarthy has since then joined the APC and had brought three bus loads of his constituents to pledge allegiance to the APC and the President. His house is used as the APC Office in Mobai. It also does not help the situation when the MP openly boasts of his links to the President. 2. His counterpart in constituency 15, Dr Brima Kamanda has been representing Sierra Leone at the Ecowas Parliament as he had done before, because ostensibly this case was unresolved. Ironically since he had stood as an independent candidate, he would have been an MP according to this ruling had he topped the APC candidate in the polls-a situation that would have meant that a man who took his opponent to court on a case that was ruled to be frivolous would become an MP because his opponent, who had done nothing wrong was caught out on a legal technicality that was not of his own making.

As a respecter of the law, one can only support an appeal and hope that several parties would be equally enraged about such unfairness. Whatever the law says, we should be mindful of the very reasons that landed us in a war brought about mainly by injustice. One may indeed be justified in saying that Mr Bumble was probably right in observing "the law is an ass" and perhaps its "eye should be open by experience"-experience of what our country has gone through-experience of the needs of our people to have a say in how they are governed.

Ponder my thoughts.

# December 9, 2013

## 2014 BUDGET: MARAH'S ARTFUL JUGGLERY

Formulating a national budget in a country like ours is an unenviable task for various reasons. Some may say it is an impossible juggling act. Expenditure not only surpasses income, but it is near to impossible to seriously address many of our socio economic challenges. Every man and his dog wants to increase the budget for his preferred area of expenditure to comply with one international or regional "declaration" or another. The Government, wanting to meet one campaign promise or another finds out that "the spirit is willing but the body is weak".

The Finance Minister, Dr. Kaifala Marah and his team have gone to great lengths to make the formulation process transparent. Participatory Budgeting, which they have emulated, is rapidly gaining attention from governments, civil society, and development agencies as an effective platform for strengthening transparency, voice, and accountability in public expenditure management, and service delivery. Indeed there was extensive consultation on the budget, although the Finance Ministry did wield its big stick to ensure that MDAs were kept in check and tailored their demands to augur with the Ministry's new thrust for budget preparation.

It would be patently unfair to pass judgment on Marrah's juggling Act because of the aforementioned difficulties. A few comments and concerns should however be in place, especially when a considerable number of novel ideas have been included into the process. Marah says that "Government has therefore dedicated this budget to the youth, women and our workforce. Hence, the Theme: "Improving the Livelihood of Youth, Women and our Workforce"." The amounts (if you were to think of them in dollars rather than trillions of Leones) are quite small. Domestic revenue is projected at Le 2.58 trillion ($593m). Of this, income taxes are projected at Le 909.9 billion ($209m)- Corporate taxes constitute nearly 30% of this and personal income taxes the rest. Goods and Services Tax (GST) are projected at Le 523.4 billion ($120m) and Customs and Excise Duties are projected at Le 650.4 billion ($149m). Total grants from our development partners will amount to Le 639.6 billion ($147m).

Here is a listing of some goodies in the budget:
1. The budget will accommodate the minimum wage of Le 480,000 per month for public sector workers and will also allow a minimal structured salary increase for higher grades in the Public Service. The minimum gross monthly salary for Teachers, Police and the Military would be Le 600,000. The gross salaries of MPs is also increased by 85 percent. Paramount Chiefs will be paid salaries as from 2014.
2. To ease the problem of transportation, the Government will procure additional One hundred new buses for the Sierra Leone Road Transport Corporation in 2014.

There are also a host of innovative ideas listed in the budget. These include:

1.             The establishment of the following new funds:
- SME Fund to support business entrepreneurial skills, innovation, expansion and development as well as Youth and Women's access to credit.
- Skills Development Fund for eligible Sierra Leoneans to undertake highly specialised skilled, technical and vocational training programmes, for example, pediatrics, heart surgery, mining engineering and aeronautical science.
- Export Diversification Fund

- Women and Youth Empowerment Fund- Government for a start is allocating Le 800 million for this.
- Transformational Development Fund - All natural resources revenues will be deposited into the TDF, which will be used to finance transformational projects, stabilize Government expenditures to save for future generations.
- Project Preparation Fund, and
- Constituency Development Fund- Government is allocating Le7.8 billion to support MPs for this.

Development Partners and the Private Sector will be asked to contribute to these Funds.

2. The government is considering issuing a two to three year bond to support the financing of infrastructure projects.
3. Le 400 million ($92,000) is also provided to the Ministry of Labour for the creation of job centres and Le 1.5 billion ($345,000) to the Ministry of Youth Affairs as Government's contribution to the World Bank supported Youth Development and Capacity Building project.
4. Government will establish a National Health Insurance Scheme and is allocating Le 3.5 billion to the Ministry of Health and Sanitation to be utilized in collaboration with NASSIT to pilot this.
5. The Ministry of Finance in collaboration with the Bank of Sierra Leone will explore the possibility of establishing Islamic Banking (non-interest banking) in the medium term.
6. Government will resuscitate the National Development Bank to facilitate medium and long-term investments especially in agro-industry and has allocated Le 2.4 billion towards this.

7. To improve on the effectiveness of the operations of Cooperatives, Government is allocating Le900 million ($207,000) to provide financial support for cooperative groups.
8. The World Bank is providing US$ 8.2 million in support of the Public Sector Pay and Performance Project. To support this programme, Government is providing an amount of Le 2.2 billion to the implementing institutions.
9. To regularize the setting of salaries and eliminate disparities in salaries across the public sector especially subvented agencies, Government will set up the Salaries and Wages Commission in 2014.

Some of the innovative ideas in the budget are certainly worthwhile but would have to be thought through carefully. Introducing too many funds at one time may prove problematic if not managed carefully. The idea of having long term bonds may be a good one as it will help government fund long term infrastructure projects. It however needs a disciplined government that will spend the monies wisely and will engender confidence in those buying such bonds that the returns will be appreciable and bonds will be redeemed without hindrance. Money provided for some of the initiatives may be ridiculous-like the $92,000 for job centres. It will also be interesting to see how Islamic banking is introduced. A lot of thought needs to be put into the operation of the Transformational Development Fund. The salary increases are welcome as long as they do not prove to be unduly inflationary. Some may say also it is a good thing to pay MPs well as long as they end up doing their jobs diligently. They will support this part of the budget-after all turkeys don't vote for Christmas!

It is also heartening to note that there is some convergence between this budget and some of the proposals in the SLPP manifesto. The SLPP manifesto also did propose special funds for women, youths and sports. In justifying the establishment of the Women's Development Fund, it was recognized that most women lack the capital to start or expand their businesses. Credit opportunities are narrow for them and business management experience limited. The SLPP manifesto also went to great lengths to propose a universal health insurance scheme. The following is stated in this manifesto: "This will entail the setting up of a Fund to be managed by a supervisory agency. This scheme will cover primary and secondary (District hospital) services. The formally employed will contribute towards a compulsory scheme (like the NASSIT scheme with employer and employee contributions). The vulnerable including minors and disabled will not make payments to the scheme but the rest of the population will contribute towards an annual premium. Additional funds will be obtained by reallocating health expenditure, part of the GST and other funds and from donor contributions. This will be gradually implemented over a four year period."

I am particularly pleased that money seems to be available for power sector reform. The budget proposes Le 35.9 billion for rebuilding the national transmission and distribution network.

The World Bank, European Commission, AfDB, IDB, EBID, United Nations Industrial Development Organisation (UNIDO) and China EximBank are providing an amount of US$ 206.9 million to support various projects in the Energy Sector, including the West African Power Pool project US$ 140.3 million; the Unbundling and Restructuring of the energy sector, US$ 54.0 million; and the rebuilding of the National Transmission and Distribution Network, US$ 11.3 million. One only hopes these will come to fruition.

It is however disconcerting, as noted in the budget statement that despite the drop in the 3-months Treasury bill rate from 19 percent in December 2012 to 3.5 percent in October 2013 and the interest rates on Treasury Bonds from 20 percent in December 2012 to 6 percent in October 2013, lending rates for commercial Banks remain high. Also the normal problems with the national budget still predominate. Consider the following absurdities:

- The tourism budget of Le 2.2 billion ($506,000) indicates we may not be that serious about developing this sector.
- Budget appropriations to Local Councils are still so low as to suggest we may be paying lip service to real decentralization.
- The budget for education is highly skewed towards tertiary education. There is very little appropriated for primary education and technical and vocational education.

One very much hoes that the strategies outlined by Government as espoused in the budget speech for domestic revenue mobilisation will be pursued with seriousness-"Domestic revenue collection efforts in 2014 and the medium term will focus on (i) broadening the tax base; (ii) reducing customs and GST duty waivers; (iii) combating tax evasion; (iv) enhancing transparency and accountability in revenue collection, (v) strengthening enforcement and compliance and (vi) strengthening revenue administration through administrative reforms including use of advanced information technology. A specialised Unit for the administration of revenues from the Extractive Industries will be established at the National Revenue Authority (NRA)."

Quite an artful juggling exercise, Dr. Marah! May the Lord bless you and keep you, as well as make your political colleagues meaningfully pursue your vision.

Ponder my thoughts.

# December 17, 2013

## LOCAL CONTENT: PANACEA FOR UNEMPLOY-MENT?

The unemployment situation is dire. Many people looking for jobs eventually give up and start pursuing some self employment scheme, often for a mere pittance. Unemployment is hard to define because of its varied forms. Data on employment rates could have severe limitations in a country like Sierra Leone because of difficulties of reflecting the high levels of various types of self-employment and the number of people living below the poverty line. There is a direct correlation between the number of people employed and the Gross Domestic Product (GDP) of a country. The unemployment rate in Sierra Leone, by whatever standards used for measurement is unacceptably high. Some 80% of the urban and rural labour force may be under-utilised. The World Bank Country Manager recently put the figure for secure employment at 3 percent and vulnerable employment at 8 percent. Whatever the exact figure, graduate and non graduate unemployment figures are clearly unacceptable.

A buoyant private sector is required to address the unemployment situation and many people see the correct implementation of the Local Content Policy as a panacea of sorts. The policy gives measures to promote the use of locally sourced goods and services and encourage employment and training of Sierra Leoneans at various managerial levels. Local content utilisation is however relatively low. One recent study concludes the utilisation of local supply varies from 0.1% in the oil & gas sector to 5.8% in mining and 45.6% in banking, with low rates mostly related to low capacity. This is not surprising as local business participation in the economy accentuates trade over manufacturing. The Mining industry in particular has an immense potential for providing employment. The multiplier effect in terms of other jobs created –suppliers, contract workers, businesses supported are immense.

Many local service providers are faced with financial and operating capacity issues. Access to capital is a major limitation in the implementation of private sector initiatives especially for Small and Medium Scale enterprises (SMEs). Despite the recent drop in the rates for treasury bills and bonds, lending rates for commercial Banks remain unacceptably high. Even though we have our labour laws (our work permit system gives preference to Sierra Leoneans), these do not work well as Government is more interested in raising revenue from the various schemes than implementing these laws. Another factor militating against greater local participation is the dearth of technical skills amongst middle level technicians. Many Sierra Leonean companies are unable to meet quality standards required by various clients. An executive of a locally based expatriate company dealing with the food industry recently expressed with surprise that local suppliers could not meet the company's requirements for poultry products. Technical standards are amongst the reasons why our companies have not fully taken advantage of the AGOA initiative.

 Local companies have also complained about cumbersome prequalification and entry requirements when bidding. Despite the fact that the LCP provides for a preferential margin of 10 per cent to domestic firms in government and private procurement, this has yet to be fully implemented. One of the biggest drawbacks is the inordinately high cost of power which makes most manufacturing undertakings by SMEs uneconomic.
These concerns have been expressed at many fora discussing the LCP. The various schemes to improve access to capital must be vigorously encouraged. These include but are not limited to lines of credit for exporters, services by Rural Banks and workable and carefully targeted micro credit schemes. The plans in the recent budget to have an SME Fund and Women and Youth Empowerment Funds should be met with cautious optimism. It

is recognised that domestic firms need to be strengthened through public private partnerships to train and build capacity to enable them to take advantage of the available opportunities.

Some companies like the Sierra Leone Brewery which uses a substantial amount of locally produced sorghum are taking advantage of the requirement to utilise locally produced inputs. There should be a conscious effort by Government to institutionalise schemes that will stimulate and expand the market for domestic products. Such schemes may include: Mandating government institutions to purchase local rice and other local foodstuffs, gearing procurement procedures for MDAs towards giving priority to local quality goods that are within acceptable pricing levels and requiring that certain specified goods like furniture should be bought locally.

There is need for upgrading the quality of technical and vocational skills. Attempts must be made at better rationalising educational courses to meet the aspirations of a development oriented job market. There is also need to enhance the capacity of women and remove impediments in order to markedly improve their participation in the informal sector .Women constitute over 50% of the population of Sierra Leone and are the backbone of the rural economy. They are however confronted by several constraints including limited access to credit and technological knowhow, relative lack of education and training and legal and cultural impediments. The Ministry of Youth affairs and the Youth Commission are doing their best to address youth employment issues and have together with other institutions developed programmes to address these issues. They are however severely constrained due to inadequate funding.

To meaningfully address the unemployment situation, the capacity and authority of the Labour Ministry should be enhanced for keeping relevant statistics on employment matters. The Ministry needs to be capacitated and empowered to play a better leading role of collating, synthesising and disseminating employment information and in carrying out its planning, regulatory and coordinating functions for employment matters. Other Ministries and appropriate agencies must be made more aware of this role and made to cooperate with the Labour Ministry in this endeavour.

It is clear that though the LCP alone will not address the unemployment situation, it is a good pedestal which will serve as a springboard for addressing many of the unemployment related problems. Clearly there is light at the end of the tunnel, but there may be a train coming from the other end, and some concerns need to be addressed. Many stakeholders are unaware of the niceties of the LCP. The coordinating office must prepare a communications strategy for outreach to communities, companies and small businesses in order to promote an understanding of local content opportunities. Transparency in implementation of the policy must be ensured and the regulatory mechanism must be clear and unequivocal. These measures, together with a well functioning inter ministerial subcommittee will go a long way towards addressing any potential problems. Such problems may also include "Reform capture" by various players for personal gain.

It is intended to have proper tools for monitoring and evaluating the implementation of the LCP. Civil society can be most useful in assisting with monitoring but would itself undoubtedly need to get to grips with the salient issues in order to maintain objectivity. In the final analysis, Government needs to have the political will to implement the Local content Policy and also widen the scope of its examination of the wider unemployment situation.

## WITCHCRAFT AND MAGIC IN PORT LOKO

There is yet another gripping story from Port Loko. Fast recovering from the aftermath of a "plane crash" involving a 15 seater "witch plane", the people of Port Loko, according to

Hassan Bruce, a reporter for the popular radio programme Monologue, have again been beset by another tragedy-this time involving magicians. The story goes that after an impressive performance by a local magician, Momoh Turay (real name withheld) in which he managed to free himself from the bondage of being tied up in a piece of tarpaulin, an out of town magician, Alucine Sesay (not actual name) promised to go one better. He caused a palm tree to grow on a barren field in the presence of gazing onlookers. Buoyed by his triumph, he asked to be tied up and thrown into the river. Several strong men gladly carried out his request and he was thrust into the river. There was however a small snag-he drowned! Trouble followed however and ten men are currently assisting police with the matter. Not surprisingly the arrest also includes the rival local magician Momoh Turay.

Several questions are now being asked: Did the appearance of a palm tree on a barren field signify the resurgence of a party (Let's also keep it nameless, shall we?) that was considered moribund in the District? Did the rival magician call on some "angels" to help tighten the knots tied around his opponent? Meanwhile investigations continue. Someone has actually opined that this may be a con trick gone awry. "He was not as smart as the South African interpreter at Mandela's funeral", he says. After being outed as a fake interpreter, Thamsamqa Jantjie said he was qualified but was disturbed by "angels". He started hearing voices in his head and hallucinating. This resulted in gestures which made no sense during the memorial. He made references to "donkeys", "lightning bolt", "prawns", and "rocking horses". At least he seemed to have got away with it.

Pity they don't have donkeys and rocking horses in Port Loko!

Ponder my thoughts.

# COMMENTS ON

# PONDER MY THOUGHTS

In this first volume of "Ponder My Thoughts", Keili affirms why many consider him a Renaissance Man-engineer, public policy wonk, politician and lay preacher. With wit and lucidity, he illuminates the challenges of life and polity in our Sierra Leone. This is a delightfully engaging read!

*Samuel Zoker*
*CEO, Western Africa Offgrid*

\*\*\*\*

This is a much needed initiative that accords Sierra Leoneans the opportunity to assess how effectively the governance architecture performs on a daily basis. The lucid commentaries shed light on the practical side of everyday life for various categories of Sierra Leoneans, bringing out the good, the bad and the ugly. Recommended reading.

*Valnora Edwin*
*National Coordinator, Campaign for Good Governance*

\*\*\*\*

Over the past few years, Andrew Keili has become one of the most respected newspaper columnists in Sierra Leone, with his weekly "Ponder My Thoughts" column being carried by all the top newspapers in the country. The reasons for this are not hard to find, for his writing seems to draw on a wide ranging life experience backed by a generous dose of literary skill.

Apart from being an engineer, Andrew is a politician, and a prominent member of the main opposition party with an eye on the presidency of the country, and so one would have thought that his writing would be overtly or covertly political in nature, but this is not the case. Even though his political leanings feature in his column from time to time, his comments easily pass the test for fairness and his own party has not been spared criticism from time to time.

Andrew's Ponder My Thoughts is a commentary on current socio-political events in Sierra Leone, but it not only has a timeless quality, it also has a universal appeal because the themes he deals with are not unique to Sierra Leone.

From a newspaper perspective, Andrew's column is an Op-Ed (Opinion Editorial) and presents the views of an individual on a particular issue. Each week, Andrew selects his topics carefully, obviously with due consideration to currency, national importance and social relevance. As a result he is able to catch the attention of the reading public, many of whom have come to respect his views, not only because of their insightfulness, but also because they are expressed with such flair.

Andrew no doubt has tremendous literary skill, which gives him the ability to be humorous or satirical from time to time, thus making the bitter pill of criticism more palatable for those who come under the glare of his pen. His criticism is also transparently constructive and draws from his wide-ranging experience in both the private and public sectors, experience which he copiously references in his writing. This places his writing firmly under the category of fair comment. So even if you disagree with his opinion, you cannot help but accept that is has been done in good faith.

In my view, it is this element of fair comment, coupled with his dexterous use of the English language, in a newspaper landscape not particularly known for consistency in grammatical accuracy, that has endeared him to the reading public.

I believe Andrew Keili's Ponder My Thoughts will continue to enlighten and entertain readers on the pages of Sierra Leonean newspapers and publication of this collection of his writings should further cement his reputation as a socio-political commentator.

I have so come to value his thoughts every week that I almost wish he loses interest in the flagbearership of his political party so I can look forward to reading Ponder My Thoughts in Premier News for a long time to come.

*Julius Spencer*
*Managing Director Premier Media Group*
*(Proprietor of Premier News newspaper)*